AS I SEE IT

By Norman Thomas

AMERICA'S WAY OUT
AS I SEE IT

AS I SEE IT

By

NORMAN THOMAS

NEW YORK
THE MACMILLAN COMPANY
1932

25

TO
F. V. T.

PREFACE

THIS collection of essays and papers must speak for itself or not speak at all. No explanatory preface can do much to help or hurt. Nevertheless there is one preliminary word I should like to say to the reader. It is this:

I am fully aware of the danger that a book containing so many references to issues and events current at the time of writing runs the risk of being even more ephemeral than the average book. On the other hand, unless we deal with current events in somewhat more permanent form than in occasional articles and speeches, we are losing still more of the fast diminishing opportunities to arrest the drift to catastrophe. It is true enough that, before this book sees the light of day, events in Manchuria and possibly also at Geneva may have written a definite chapter in terms of war or peace, armament or disarmament, on which I now can only speculate. Yet I cannot imagine any likely events which will alter the lessons I want to draw from the direction of drift in these confused and troublous times. It is, moreover, my very deep conviction that especially in the year of a national electoral campaign it is of the highest importance for any man who wants to speak on politics at all to speak in clear-cut terms concerning present issues. It is in this conviction that

I commit this book to the tender mercies of the public. Will my hoped-for readers please consider that in one important sense this is an effort to bring up to date the position I have set forth in *America's Way Out: A Program for Democracy?*

Much of this material has appeared in articles or has been used in speeches. In every case, however, these papers in their present form represent some degree of revision. In most cases that revision amounts to a very considerable re-writing or expansion of the original article or speech. My thanks are due to the *New Republic,* the *Atlantic Monthly,* the *Forum,* and the *Christian Century* for permission to use material which I had already published in their columns. Two of the papers are revisions and expansion of speeches— one made at the Smith College Commencement in 1931 and the other at the Williamstown Institute of Politics in the same summer. My thanks are also due to my wife for her interested hearing and criticism of these pages in their various stages of production, and to Miss Freda Straus for typing the manuscript, often in the midst of many interruptions.

NORMAN THOMAS.

November 13, 1931.

CONTENTS

AS I SEE IT

RECONSIDERATIONS

A YEAR or more ago I wrote a book—not an uncommon offense in America—less as a final, magisterial program for our times than as a stimulant to a discussion of a more comprehensive philosophy and plan than Americans generally had considered. This book with the confident title *America's Way Out: A Program for Democracy* was, on the whole, better received than I had hoped; that is, there were more reviews and more friendly reviews than I had expected. Nevertheless I was disappointed by the nature of the reviews, and such of the more informal discussion of the book as reached my ear. Briefly, it seemed to me that the discussion missed the mark because it went off in broad generalizations, favorable or unfavorable to this or that position of mine, rather than in argument about the basic and desperately important issues I was discussing. Yet that very fact is significant and has weight in any reconsideration of the American scene.

The reviews I saw dated themselves and the book with a vengeance. They were written in the midst of an economic depression which was getting worse and not better. A criticism of the existing order which would have been ignored or laughed at by men who thought that they and everybody else could get rich by taking a flier in Wall Street (even if they couldn't find work) was assured a respectable hearing by the depression. Indeed if I were a captain of industry concerned for the intellectual defense of capitalism, I should worry about that portion of our intelligentsia which reviews books. The best that any reviewer could say for the system I criticized was a more or less formal disclaimer of complete agreement with my criticisms. Some of them seemed annoyed that I did not curse the capitalist devils harder or at any rate louder. One suspects, however, that if the turn of the business cycle brings even a moderate boom some reviewers will want to do a little reconsidering on their own account of an attitude that is largely emotional, born of the immediate situation rather than any real conviction.

In the run of papers and magazines the reviewers fell into two classes, both of which for different reasons found my remarks "mild" or "moderate," not "genuine Socialism"—at least of the pre-war brand—or just "common sense." The first of these groups, and much the larger, illustrated the abysmal ignorance even of literate Americans concerning socialism. Socialism, these reviewers seemed to think, always shrieks. If a socialist talks less than bloody revolution around the next corner, virtue has gone out of him. The exceedingly moderate record of the German Social Democrats or the British Labor Party—too lacking

in boldness of plan and vigor of execution—is wasted
on them. For them Henri de Man, the Webbs, the
Shaw of *The Intelligent Woman's Guide to Socialism
and Capitalism*, the most recent G. D. H. Cole, and
Kautsky, the critic of communism, have not written.
Otherwise their astonishment at the moderation of a
program at many points much in advance of what
British and continental socialists have said and done
would have been impossible.

The second group, smaller in number, was more
sophisticated. Its members know more about socialism and communism, but some of them belong to that
particular brand of parlor radicals who found esoteric
reasons for voting for Al Smith (if they voted at all)
in 1928, who hold down the best jobs they can get,
and then occasionally talk a vehement or cynical
radicalism. Naturally they rationalize their position
by finding socialism too tame, and by discovering
agreements between my program and the position of
such diverse citizens as Al Smith, George W. Norris,
and Owen D. Young which these gentlemen have
carefully concealed from the world.

Whatever the reasons for the tone of the reviews it
must be said that evidently most editors give their reviewers a free hand—perhaps they don't read their
columns. At any rate only a few short days after the
literary lady who does books for that strong tower of
conservatism, the Chicago *Tribune*, had discovered
me surprisingly sensible and not very "subversive,"

the good old editorial columns thundered once more
against one of the smaller parts of the program out-
lined in my book. I was denounced for my internationalism as I had been denounced for my opposition
to the power trust. Thus may an author be moderate
to reviewers when his principles and program excite
owners and editors to a great rage in defense of "our
American institutions" of which the most sacred is
private profit. It is a fair conclusion that it will be a
long time before the reviewers' conception of what is
"mild" and "moderate" weakens the resistance of editors and other propagandists of the status quo to all
but trifling and belated concessions to the needs of the
masses.

Among many socialists and radicals there was, as I
expected, some disapproval of my lack of orthodox
Marxism which so far, with few exceptions, has found
expression in general reaffirmation of faith rather in
specific answer to the points I raised. Some critics
took occasion, again in terms of affirmation rather
than argument, to deride all hope of comparatively
orderly and peaceful social revolution. One of these,
writing in an excellent journal of exceedingly limited
circulation among the intelligentsia, a paper now un-
fortunately dead, was especially sure that what I said
could have no appeal to the producing masses, his own
contacts with the aforesaid masses being largely derived from lectures before women's clubs on life and
literature, with especial reference to sex. It is fair to

add that the limitation of space at a reviewer's disposal doubtless explains in part the deficiency of argument of which I have complained. All of which is by way of explaining my comparative disappointment at the quality of discussion which I evoked. Nevertheless, as a result of that discussion, and of my own thinking in the light of the development of the last twelve months, there are certain considerations and reconsiderations of the way out for America—and the world—which I should like to set down.

1. First of all, if I were writing to-day I should add an even stronger note of urgency. If we are to avoid catastrophe there is no time to lose. Each month that we drift increases the likelihood of a confused, violent catastrophic breakdown of a politico-economic system already creaking under heaped-up strains. It will not do to tell us that America lived through as bad an economic depression in the seventies and the nineties. There were for us fewer foreign complications then, there was no Russian Five-Year Plan and there was a less general conviction of the utter needlessness of poverty in a world of such actual and potential producing power. We may, probably we shall, if Europe is kept from complete collapse, come out of this periodic crisis of overproduction, or rather underconsumption, into better times, without, however, getting real prosperity or economic security for the workers. The kind of comfort which assures us that having survived the measles, whooping cough and scarlet fever, we shall

probably survive diphtheria only to have the smallpox seven years later is cold comfort indeed.

In the face of a situation even worse than it seemed a year ago there has been a greater paralysis of effective action. The British financial crisis, even more than the German, has brought home to us how near is Europe to the brink of ruin. The catastrophe we fear will not be a brief prelude to something as relatively orderly or hopeful as the Russian dictatorship now affords. It is more likely to mean at least a generation of utter confusion, of foreign and civil wars fought with all the devilish ingenuity of science, of strife between bewildering and shifting alignments of men basically loyal to conflicting ideals of nationalism, internationalism, the older capitalism, fascism, socialism and communism. Hence the urgency of stressing constructive forces and a program.

2. If I were to-day rewriting a program for our American democracy I should give more space and emphasis to the immediate emergency at hand. We face a third winter of unemployment, involving if not an increase, certainly no great diminution of a tragic army of the jobless now estimated at some 10,-000,000 adults, a great many of them with children for whom they are responsible. Farming, especially wheat farming, is in the doldrums. Wheat last summer was selling at twenty-five and thirty cents in Kansas, so much less than the cost of production for most farmers that some of it was not harvested. There is

every sign of an actual overproduction of wheat in the world, at least in relation to effective demand. The success of the collectives in Russia may spell the ultimate doom of individual, small-scale wheat farming even in the United States. But the wheat or cotton grower who gives up and goes to the city runs the hazard of joining the jobless without even a patch of ground to raise foodstuffs or a shelter over his head. The decline in the price level, especially in agriculture, means that the farmer is paying back his mortgages with dollars worth at least twenty to twenty-five cents more than when he borrowed his money. The tenant farmers who are the most miserable and the most ignored of all farmers could not survive at all save that the emergency has forced an uneven and informal moratorium on rent. But then debts pile up!

Still worse is a condition of a third great group of producers: the coal miners. Thousands of them live under feudal conditions in lonely camps where their only shelter is company-owned shacks, in many of which a self-respecting farmer would hesitate to keep a cow. For these shacks and for provisions bought at company stores at prices from fifteen to fifty per cent above the average, pay is deducted out of wages for the part-time work which is all the miners can get. I have seen stacks of pay slips showing no balance at all in cash for the worker at the end of two weeks and sometimes even a deeper indebtedness to the company. For these miners there is added to the semi-starvation which they share with the unemployed or irregularly employed, a serfdom unmatched in America save possibly in some textile villages. No wonder there are strikes which will grow grimmer and more violent.

Yet deep as may be the crimes and blunders of the operators the trouble essentially is with a sick industry which must adjust itself to the advance in machinery, to the use of oil, and to increasing electrification, without plan, without the stabilizing influence of a strong union, under a system of chaotic competition.

Let us add, to complete the picture, that the railroads, having reduced the number of their employees to the limit of safety, sought a fifteen per cent increase in freight rates on goods which at present prices scarcely can find buyers. They did not get this increase but got from the Interstate Commerce Commission some rate increases to form a pool to be shared in communistic fashion by the roads.

The approach to these diverse yet interrelated miseries is haphazard. There is no general plan. No one in authority discusses a way to bring order and health to the coal industry. That would mean socialization of coal as a condition, and the very word is anathema to all except those operators who want to palm off on the public their unprofitable properties at high prices. Only here and there do a few bold voices, echoing Commissioner Eastman, point to the plight of the railroads as showing the need of a unified social control going beyond regulation and rate tinkering.

The farmers, to be sure, have the Farm Board to relieve them either of their poverty or their farms— they are not sure which—but suspect the latter, and rend the heavens with their well-grounded complaints. Yet neither they nor their political friends have as yet proposed a plan to meet this emergency which will not commit us to subsidizing uneconomic production, or to dumping wheat and cotton abroad at grave danger to world trade and world peace, or simply destroying part of these crops. Now, however, the farmers are beginning to say, with justice, that if it is to the inter-. est of the world to wipe out, scale down, or, at any rate, postpone the payment of German government debts, a somewhat similar moratorium might be arranged on farm rents and mortgages or, still better, they might be readjusted in the light of the increased purchasing power of the dollar.

The best plan of all would be to restore the price level of 1927. The price level is affected by international forces and could best be raised by international action, but I think action by the Federal Reserve Board, loans for unemployment relief and other measures of carefully guarded inflation here in America, are definitely in order and alone promise help to the farmers. Certainly any plan which would intelligently lighten the burden of debt on agriculture and industry is preferable to any scheme of debentures which would only work by encouraging dumping; that is, the sale of American grain cheaper abroad than at home.

Europe, if she had a shortage of wheat might welcome such an arrangement, but in the intense competition for wheat markets since the recovery not only of Russia but of other wheat areas such dumping would seriously affect good relations between nations. Witness our own excitement about Russian dumping!*

But more important even then help for branches of agriculture, going through a difficult period of readjustment owing to the combination of mechanical improvement and a declining rate of increase in population, is help for the unemployed. Already public funds are estimated to bear about 70 per cent of the cost of organized relief. Some cities—by no means all —have come dangerously near the line of increasing their tax rates to a point which threatens small house owners with foreclosure. Since our cities can only raise funds by an unscientific tax on real estate which does not discriminate between land and improvements, the city is about the worst taxing agency on which to depend for emergency relief. The federal government is the best, first, because it has power (which many states and all cities lack) to tax incomes and inheritances, and do it equitably for the whole country; and second, because the depression is nationwide and should be dealt with on that basis.

----

*The months since these paragraphs were written have seen a growth of sentiment among farmers for government agencies to purchase and market at a fixed price commodities necessary for domestic use. The plan has difficulties, but also possibilities under proper administration. Like most plans for the help of one group it will work hardship to others unless it is part of a plan for general socialization of production and marketing. Unless it is accompanied or rapidly followed by proper taxation of land values it will start new land booms and pour most of its benefits in the laps of the land owners.

In the unnecessary war against Germany, from the disastrous consequences of which we still suffer, the nation raised some $21,500,000,000 in "liberty" loans. This went to the work of destruction. No banker or economist offered objection. Yet the propertied classes are desperately afraid of a $5,000,000,000 hunger loan—such as the Socialists proposed long before William Randolph Hearst! This loan should be repaid out of income and inheritance taxes (or if necessary out of a capital levy) and the proceeds of it be used for a larger program of public works. First place in such a program I should give to a frontal attack on the "sub-standard" housing in which one-third of our people live. Most of the great loan should be reloaned to public housing authorities, federal or municipal, to provide low price housing at cost. Public credit would be behind these loans, but most if not all of them could be repaid under a proper plan. Another part of the loan might well be spent on such a productive enterprise as the electrification of rural areas under a public authority. In every possible way the loan should be so administered as to fit into a program of socialization. If it is only regarded as oxygen for a dying capitalism it will merely postpone the day of reckoning. It can be used to remove the worst of our menacing slums, to provide work and to stimulate enterprise.

No serious argument has been advanced against this plan. It would not cause unwholesome inflation. If it helped restore the price level of 1925-1927 that would be a good thing. It would not take money away from industry that needs it. In a time of overproduction, not industry but consumption needs financing. There is no dearth of money at low rates for sound investment. If our rulers refuse to consider this plan of a hunger loan or if it does not work, they may find themselves forced to choose between subsidizing consumers on a great scale, letting them starve or shooting them when they riot. There is evidence that some of our masters may not be averse to the last method of relieving hunger.

The present emergency also calls attention to the shocking weakness of our banking system. Among other specific measures that I should advocate, were I to-day writing an immediate program, would be a requirement that all commercial banks be put under federal rather than state control and compelled to belong to the Federal Reserve system. Not only in percentage of failures but in tragic results, the state banks (headed by the Bank of United States in New York City as the largest single failure in our history) have greatly exceeded the national bank failures. In the years 1926-1930 there were 6,987 bank suspensions of which 5,806 were state banks not members of the Federal Reserve system and 257 state banks members of the system. Moreover, the banking situation requires uniform, national control.

I should also strongly favor the proposal made in more detail by Professor Colston Warne at a recent

L. I. D. conference for a development of the Postal
Savings Bank system as a general federal bank for both
commercial and properly segregated savings accounts.
The post offices could still be convenient agencies of
branch banks but the system would have its own board
of control. It could be a beginning of a socialized
banking system. Nothing less than such a system can
solve the problem of money, banking and credit. To-
day our great banking groups skim the cream off the
national earnings without guaranteeing any protection
to depositors in banks which may fail.*

3. Of course any reconsideration of a book a year
old which mentions Russia must take account of developments in that remarkable land. I do not find
much that I would change in the main lines of my discussion of Russia and of communism. The progress
of collectivized farming within the year has made the
success of the bold and ruthless effort to break up the
old agricultural way of life more nearly certain than
when I wrote. On the other hand Stalin's further
recession toward capitalist devices of unequal pay and
unequal rewards for work of varying value proves that
mankind cannot be pitchforked into absolute economic equality or coerced into good work but must
at the most hopeful best be reëducated. There is, how-

---

*Since this was written, the President and Congress have set up the great two
billion dollar Reconstruction Finance Corporation. It may have been a necessary
move, but coming from advocates of "rugged individualism" it is an overwhelming
proof of the breakdown of their own system and the need for government in business.
At the least, the law should have provided safeguards against bolstering up watered
stock and labor baiting corporations and it should have given the public a voice in the
banks and businesses it is compelled to save.

ever, nothing fatal to socialism in the degree of inequality of reward Stalin has recognized. Ownership is still social; men in Russia cannot live by their claims on what everyone needs to use. Private profit is not lord of economic life.

On the whole, with all due allowance for food and other shortages, the year would seem to give an increasing verdict of success to the Russian experiment in two great particulars: (1) The Soviet government has made astonishing progress in setting up a planned national economy and in explaining it to the people of its own country and the world; for example, through such books as *New Russia's Primer,* so popular in America; (2) Russia is disproving the fallacy of the necessity of the lordship of the profit motive to make men work and work hard.

On the third matter vital to the socialist: the increase of liberty, the Russian record is far less good and the application of the Russian method in America with her traditions would be impossible unless our present spirit should be utterly broken by terrific disaster. Imagine coercing 1,000,000 American farmers as the Russian Kulaks were coerced! Despite this, however, communism and particularly communistic unions in the United States have made some progress within the year, a progress due partly to their own devoted, sometimes foolish, and always intolerant, energy and effort, and partly to the apathy or worse of many of the regular unions. It remains to be seen how much they can hold of the ground they are slowly gaining.

Finally the Soviet government has persisted in paths of international peace during the year, has refrained from the temptation to aid communist revolt in the German crisis, and has actually taken the wind out of its capitalist neighbors' sails by proposing, as it once proposed disarmament, an economic treaty against dumping "with teeth in it." Mr. Hamilton Fish's fears are not justified.

4. The last of these brief reconsiderations must take account of the quality of my Marxism for which I have been criticized by friends whose judgment I respect. I confess I have seen no reason to alter the position I took in writing on a socialist philosophy. I believe there is such a philosophy that goes deeper than pragmatism, a philosophy that approaches a kind of religion of liberty, equality and fraternity. I believe that the appeal of such a philosophy is ethical, but not in any sense which sets ethics apart from life and the developing economics of our time. Certainly it is not a philosophy without power or one which appeals only to a generalized reason and goodwill. It appeals very definitely and specifically to the exploited workers with hand and brain throughout the world.

In the historical development of socialism, Marx and the Marxist school hold first place. Marx so bestrides our modern world that in the realm of politics and economics men are judged by the general attitude they take to the cause of which he was so mighty a leader and teacher. It is increasingly coming to pass, almost to the degree that it came to pass with Jesus and Paul, that for practical purposes what Marx and Engels actually said and meant is less important for the world than what the various churches, or rather parties, which call themselves Marxists, say they said and meant. In a practical sense Marx will mean what the strongest church says that he means. To-day there is sharp division on that point between socialists and communists who are equally firm believers. If either wins a complete victory or if both continue, it will not necessarily prove of itself which, if either, has been right in interpreting the mind of Marx, any more than the relative strength of Catholic and Protestant churches in the sixteenth century proved which, if any, of the warring sects correctly interpreted primitive Christianity. Nevertheless discussion of Marxism is in order and I shall briefly recapitulate my position.

The Marxian theory of crisis finds immense confirmation in the present depression, and the Marxian prophecy of the destruction of capitalism, when its work was done, by the doom it carried within it, is being fulfilled before our eyes. That doom may have been delayed; when it comes it may be more largely due to the stupid and blind psychology of an acquisitive society and to its nationalistic follies and less to its pure economic weakness than early Marxists thought, but doom it surely will be.

The economic interpretation of history is the most useful single theory we have for historical interpretation and forecast. My objection to extravagant claims for it is that we cannot work it in the laboratory of life as we work scientific laws in chemistry. Still less can we make it, in these times of revolutionary change in science, psychology and philosophy, a satisfactory metaphysics. That is one point at issue between myself and some of my Marxist friends and critics. Dr. Sidney Hook, in his brilliant paper *Towards the Understanding of Karl Marx,* argues that Marxism must be interpreted as a method of social revolution and not as an exact science of social prediction. To the degree that he is right—and his paper is critical of all schools of Marxists—my criticism is relatively unimportant. It is not unimportant in the light of popular Marxism.

Another and more serious point concerns the class struggle. I believe not only in the obvious fact of struggle between groups with conflicting economic interest, but in *the* class struggle between an owning and a working class. That struggle is evident all round the world. It explains the bitterness of American strikes and the worst defects of American justice. The idea of such a struggle is or may be a unifying force in asserting the international solidarity of labor. But I protest when certain self-proclaimed Marxists act as if to believe in the class struggle was a kind of mystic act of salvation by faith, which almost absolves them from hard and intelligent work to organize labor economically or politically, or from the effort to purge labor unions from exceedingly "capitalistic" abuses, and which permits them to fight communism far more enthusiastically than capitalism. I protest when other Marxists act as if the proclamation of the class struggle were enough automatically to teach and inspire the workers to know how to deal with the prejudices and problems of our difficult times. Actually the idea of class solidarity of workers of different races, colors, nations and economic conditions, however much it conforms to the deepest reality, is an ethical ideal needing to be taught and explained. And the wisdom to guide the reshaping of our society does not come from mere affirmation of the differing interest of owners and workers.

There is, I repeat, a tremendous service an understanding of the class conflict can give us in saving us from merely Utopian appeals to general goodwill and in driving us to a proper organization and education of the class on which we must depend. Recognition of it is basic to a Socialist Party. But even at this point a few words of practical warning are in order.

The socialist ideal, as distinguished from the communist, is social salvation *without* catastrophe, and with a minimum of confusion and disorder. This was essentially as true in action of the socialism of Hardie and Bebel and Jaurès as of their post-war successors. Socialism is not committed to absolute democracy or absolute pacifism regardless of time, place and circumstance, but in our western world socialism seeks earnestly to preserve international peace and to utilize democratic methods. Now these things are consistent with the class struggle, but not with such exclusive concentration on the class struggle that we turn it into class war and lose sight of the other appeal to that important minority of men and women who can transcend immediate class or group interest for the sake of freedom, peace and plenty in a world now in terrible danger of cataclysmic disaster. Not vengeance on a middle class but absorption of it into a classless world of prosperous workers for the common good is our socialist hope. In trying times like these not only that part of the middle class which is struggling with increasing difficulty to maintain its precarious foothold, but those in its ranks still economically secure, may have more than an esthetic or ethical interest in the crusade for peace and economic security and freedom. Their help is not to be despised or needlessly alienated. The plain fact is that in the curious American scene to-day with its peculiarly backward labor organization, the socialist and working class movement gets a valuable degree of help, intellectual, moral and financial, from within the middle class. We shall not more speedily win the workers by rejecting that help.

Here in America there is no time to lose if we want to get, not one hundred per cent correct theory, but action to avert war and disaster. Such action to be effective requires a socialist philosophy, that is, a philosophy of coöperation for the common good rather than private profit; the more explicit that philosophy the better. Certainly such action requires us to get conscious working class support. But it does not require a socialist *creed*, worked out in detail, which compels every speech and every speaker to shout class conflict in Marxist language. I think that in some degree the comparative failure of the Socialist Party in America has been due to its iteration of dogmas in terms that were not self-explanatory and which antagonized farmers, intellectuals and the majority of wage workers who would have been with us if they had understood. Our immediate business is to unite in a party, socialist in objective and program whatever its name, the men and women who want substantially what we want but go on voting for a Norris or a La Follette in the old parties because they admire them and understand their language as they do not understand us. These men in the old parties never can achieve what we want. We need our own army, but we cannot dictate to our natural friends just how they and we shall come together. We cannot wisely close all the many roads to the socialist idea except the road of class conflict. That force has not automatically united workers regardless of race, nationality, trade or wage. Of itself alone it has not taught the Russian masses the way to plan for the common good. That has been the work of a party with a high percentage of intellectuals who have used the class struggle as a unifying idea to preach. Since this is so, since the business of building a strong Socialist Party, not owned by big business, is so difficult and so urgent, since we cannot build as did our English comrades out of unions already strongly organized, but must use a varied appeal, let us not make Marxism a kind of slogan of salvation which men must accept in our precise formula before they can make socialism the alternative to disaster.

Our hope of being anything more than a Marxian sect, rather than a party, less intolerant and also less vigorous than the communists, our hope of seeing the Socialist Party escape the fate of the old Socialist Labor Party, lies in an emphasis on unity of action for immediate measures reaching toward a socialist goal. This is not to make the mistake of saying that socialism is merely the sum total of measures of socialization. It is a way of life, a philosophy, a vision of a cooperative, classless world. But it is a philosophy that must find expression and clarification in immediate and well thought out action by means which lie at our hand.

Whether they are the best interpreters of Marx or not, the communists are bound to win any rivalry of "revolutionary" devotion to class *war*. They can beat us in vehemence, they can claim a more consistent devotion in action to this single principle than the social democratic parties of Europe, and they have the tremendous influence of Russia behind them. Practically the road of exclusive insistence on class

war as the first and last commandment of Marx in
our day and in our country will lead to communism,
not to some militant new labor movement. It will
lead to war and dictatorship; not to peace and a wiser
democracy. We ought to choose with our eyes open
and this fact before them. My own choice is for
trying more effectively than ever before to bring men
to socialism by all the many appeals which make it the
only hope of our age. Of these appeals the recognition of the inevitable class conflict in a capitalist
society is one and a vitally important one, the value of
which will best be shown by our skill and energy in
trying to realize in point of fact the solidarity of the
workers with hand and brain in political and industrial action so effectively that within a generation the
cruel division of men into owners and workers shall
have perished from the earth.

Even as I write these words I realize that each
month makes my hope harder of fulfillment by the
road I want to see men travel. Perhaps only an intolerant religious dogmatism, not a scientific approach
to our problems, will pull us through the days of
social and psychological upheaval that lie ahead. If
so, it is well that that dogmatism has as much corre-
spondence to reality as all versions of Marxism have.
At least by such Marxism we may be delivered from
the sheer demagoguery, the pathetic trust in a panacea or a Messiah, of much untaught radicalism.

Nevertheless, however powerful it is, I do not think

any binding dogmatism adequate to the deepest needs of men in these revolutionary times. Its triumphs may bring us some deliverance and yet entail a need for a desperate struggle for the intellectual liberty on which social progress and individual happiness ultimately depend. While therefore it is still possible I shall urge the value of a philosophy of coöperation rather than a creed of absolute intellectual conformity as the bond of union and the source of inspiration for those who would build the new temple of humanity ere we be destroyed in the catastrophic ruin of the old.

THE NEXT DECADE

No GIFT or prophecy was ever bestowed on me at birth: I am no seventh son of a seventh son, vouchsafed visions denied other mortals. But I have had many opportunities for observing the American scene and forming some judgment on American tendencies and American public opinion—or rather public opinions. These are my credentials for a modest effort to predict—not the ultimate fate of our society—but its probable development within the next decade. I say "probable" not only out of a decent sense of my own limitations as a prophet, but also because I do not believe that there are laws, or at any rate laws that man has discovered, which work with that degree of certainty which applies in the physical laboratory. There is an area which may be small but is of fundamental significance in which the creative intelligence of the human will may operate in the collective affairs of men. It is to this and only to this that any appeal can be taken. And in the effectiveness of this appeal is the hope for mankind. What I say, therefore, of the consequences of drift is not affirmed as an inevitable fate but as the probable result of forces and tendencies now operative, a fate which can be averted or mitigated by intelligent and organized action.

Continuance of the present drift means catastrophe; probably within the decade new world war, but prior to that and even if that should be avoided, growing unrest, discontent, disorder, riots and perhaps positive revolt here in the United States. But not within this decade will there be successful social revolution unless possibly out of world war. Any approximation to social revolution will within this period be fascist rather than communist. That is to say, it will be stridently nationalist and on the whole, despite some demagoguery and a few concessions to the masses, compatible with the existence of the profit system and capitalist control of key industries and services. It will have to make some attempt at economic planning and provide at least a semblance of economic security to the masses, but this may be done for a time at a comparatively cheap price. No fascist dictatorship is likely to last long because it will leave the fundamental economic problem of equitable distribution unsolved, and without the solution of that problem there can be neither security nor peace.

I have here used the word "revolution" in the narrower significance of a dramatic, violent extra-legal overturn of government. In the larger sense of the word we cannot ask: shall we expect revolution? We live now in the midst of changes so profound as to be genuinely revolutionary in the realm of thought, politics, economics and social institutions. The sole question is: Can we so guide and direct these changes that an extremely violent revolution or attempt at revolution can be avoided? It certainly will not be avoided if things drift, even although within the decade the revolutionary attempt may be unsuccessful.

Let us look at the situation beginning with the United States, ignoring for the time being the possibility or probability of world war.

We are face to face, as I write, with the coming of the worst winter in America's peacetime history—worst not simply because of the extent of misery (perhaps that will be no greater proportionately than in other memorable years of depression) but because of the growing knowledge of the sufferers that their misery is solely due to human failure to manage properly the machinery that might provide abundance for all. We face this tragedy, moreover, without much more than a chemical trace of any widely held program or organization in which might be reasonable hope.

Nothing is clearer than that laissez-faire capitalism has broken down. At Indianapolis President Hoover saw a vision of America again on the highroad of prosperity by the working of the business cycle and as the result of individual energy. This planless progress he was bold to call the American Plan! Now it is possible that without any plan or purpose other than drift and endurance we shall sooner or later emerge from the trough of the present depression. But we shall not soon come again to another Golden Age on Wall

Street. That gold turned out to be mostly tinsel. During the height of the gambling mania, technological unemployment was increasing, the wealth of the farmers was relatively and absolutely declining, such basic industries as coal and textiles were almost mortally sick, the excessive profit to be made out of the call money market kept investors out of the field of moderate priced housing—the one building field not overdeveloped—and the banks went mad on the wild cat financing which involved hundreds of them in grief as soon as the boom broke. The circumstances which made for the structure of a seeming and partial prosperity on such foundations no longer exist and will not soon recur. There is, for instance, no chance of the kind of foreign trade we enjoyed during the reign of the lucky King Calvin nor is there any big new industry to be built up by installment sales as was the automobile industry after the World War.

These things are generally recognized by the more thoughtful in capitalist ranks. Witness the vogue for books, speeches, magazines and articles on economic plans and planning, Russian or American. Nevertheless, whatever chance the New Capitalism may have had to be our savior—and I was always among the skeptics—it has lost by its failure to do anything either of itself or through its political influence in this crisis. If it were not so tragic that failure would be ludicrous. Mr. Lincoln Steffens observed that with the Hoover election the government at Washington ceased to be the kept woman of big business and became its legal wife. But neither husband nor wife, despite the helpful hints of various volunteer planners like Dean Donham of Harvard, Nicholas Murray Butler, Stuart Chase, Professor Charles Beard, and Gerard Swope has done anything adequate, imaginative or compelling. Business and political leaders have thought and acted mostly in terms of negatives: reduction of income taxes in 1930, no "hunger loan" to match war loans, no compulsory state unemployment insurance, no articulate and coördinate plan about anything. at home or abroad. Congress accepted a one year's moratorium on the old war debts with a declaration against any further reduction of them. Yet even Congressmen must know that we cannot collect those debts and would not accept them if paid in goods in competition with our own industries!*

It is a corollary of this incapacity of our real rulers that the two major parties which by and large are their property (or—shall we say?—their political brokers in dealing with the masses) are destitute of ideas and ambition save to get and keep office. It is amazing in times like these to examine the speeches of the supposedly liberal aspirants for power in both old parties. Democratic aspirants for the Presidency, from Roosevelt to Ritchie, talk state rights and other things wise, not so wise and plain foolish, but of

*This was written before the so-called Hoover program of which the chief item is the Reconstruction Finance Corporation was adopted. The program is terribly belated, grossly inadequate and open to positive criticisms at which I have hinted in a footnote to an earlier chapter.

the pressing problems of an interdependent world, of the necessity at least for a national economy they give little hint. They have not even got around to a clear-cut demand for unemployment insurance. Despite the seriousness of the emergency and the widespread discontent, there is little chance that the Democratic platform of 1932 will be as radical as the Bryan platform of 1896. There is less chance that within the decade either old party will become the vehicle of a powerful and intelligent nationwide political protest. Not only are they too firmly controlled by an alliance of their big business financiers and the politician brokers; they are also rendered impotent by the soul destroying force of their own traditions, especially, in the case of the Democrats, by their anti-Negro complex in the South. The most we can expect is some local progressivism within the old parties—as now—and possibly within the decade some demogogic gestures on the part of one of them in the national field.

Even more serious an obstacle to sound social progress simply by drift or by the natural development of existing forces is the state of the official labor movement embodied in the A. F. of L. It stands bravely for no wage cuts and talks about shorter hours, but has thus far lacked the morale and the organization to make strikes against wage cuts or for shorter hours effective. In such dramatic and significant struggles as that last winter in Danville, Virginia, the strike lost whatever chance it had of success in these times because the A. F. of L. was not organized properly to feed its soldiers in the front-line trenches. The almost complete breakdown of the once powerful United Mine Workers Union in the bituminous field, a breakdown in morale, organization and every other quality under the much hated Lewis administration, has already turned that sick industry over to the operators whose power is tempered by their own weakness, by spontaneous revolt and recently by the rise of new unions, one communist, the other radical but not communist.

Politically A. F. of L. leaders are usually (there are, of course, honorable exceptions) in the bog of machine politics up to their necks. In the field of public affairs their outstanding spokesman, Matthew Woll, who is also acting president of the National Civic Federation, has three great issues: higher tariffs and stricter exclusion of immigrants; world boycott against Russia; and a get-together conference with employers on economic planning. His zeal in the first two matters makes him more reactionary than the intelligent capitalist; his own attitude, the weakness of the A. F. of L. and the nature of the situation make his proposed conference from the standpoint of the workers pretty much like a conference of wolves and sheep on better pasturage for sheep and better mutton for the wolves. The essentials of the profit system will not be touched. Indeed the chief passion of the A. F. of L. heirarchy is repeal of the Volstead Act.

Men who cannot buy bread will buy beer perhaps on the installment plan, and we shall float to prosperity on a sea of legal liquor.

Within a decade labor organization will probably be on a much sounder basis either through a thorough-going reform of the A. F. of L. or through the rise of new unions, or both. But neither now nor in any near future can we expect the A. F. of L. to play the rôle in aggressive but relatively orderly social progress that unions should play and to no small extent have played in Great Britain, and even at some junctures in our own country.

But this weakness of strong organizations, political or industrial, to put power behind the demands of the workers and to shape in more or less orderly fashion the demands of the unemployed, the distressed farmers, and the exploited workers, under a system which does not even assure them bread, does not mean that we may expect the continuance of the amazing docility of the first year and a half of the great depression. Indeed, as I write there are strikes in the coal regions and in some textile centers which are omens of what we may expect. Men will not and should not starve in silence to please the comfortable. If there are not strong organizations at hand which they can use they will instead turn to violent demonstrations. This happened in the terrible depression of the seventies, it will happen again.

Of organized groups with some definite philosophy

and program the communists are likely to profit or seem to profit most by the immediate effects of this rising tide of discontent. In many ways they will deserve what they will gain among the masses. Despite all their mistakes, their poverty thus far of first-rate leadership, their genius for schism in their own ranks, their lack of appreciation of American psychology, their use of lies and slanders as ordinary weapons of controversy, and their tendency to subordinate unions, strikes and all else to party needs, their own energy, plus the apathy or worse of most of the rest of us, have given them again the chance which, even after the depression began, they seemed definitely to have lost.

This is not the place to discuss the strength and weakness of communism in general or American communism in particular. Instead I am interested in pointing out some features of the American scene which make it likely that the propaganda of violence and some future revolutionary movement is more likely to serve the cause of an American fascism than of communism, at least within the decade, always provided that new world war does not upset all calculations. The outstanding reason for this prediction is the nature of the untaught American radicalism. There is plenty of it in a country where farmers got twenty-five cents a bushel for wheat in the summer of 1931 and there are ten million unemployed. But it is illiterate, dominated by a yearning for the days when the little man had his chance, complicated in many cases by race prejudice, and almost uniformly nationalistic. It is always likely to waste its energies in some quack remedy like curing all our ills by tinkering with money—witness the reappearance of Coin Harvey on the political scene.

Illustrations fairly leap to one's mind. Your Bleases, Bilbos and Heflins of the South have risen by exploiting the radicalism of the hill billy with his well justified grievances against the older plantation aristocracy and the newer business plutocracy. But such radicalism is demagogic, unintelligent and dangerously vitiated by its prejudice against the still worse exploited Negro.

Your Kansas farmer with a bumper wheat crop on his hands or your Oklahoma farmer who has found or hopes to find oil can beat any Communist cussing Wall Street and the trusts. But does he want international agreement on wheat production or nationalization and scientific control of oil production? Not by all the gods of the pioneers who saw in national resources something to be exploited as fast as possible by the finder!

The limitations on this agrarian radicalism are, of course, the limitations of a narrow class or group interest. These men still own something, and their grievance is not against capitalism but big capitalists. They fight a losing battle against an economic movement toward concentration almost as relentless as the tides, but during the next decade they will still have some strength which in the pinch can be mobilized politically for action far more like fascism than socialism or communism. The passion of little merchants against chain stores is another illustration of a discontent which has or may have political significance of a retrogressive rather than a constructively radical kind.

The interesting thing about it is that to so large a degree workers and tenant farmers who do not have the same interests as these little merchants and land owners can be made to sympathize with them. American workers have shown that they can be instinctively and violently class conscious in certain great and dramatic strikes, but it will take some years of the negative teaching of bitter experience and positive education in constructive radicalism to eradicate the bourgeois philosophy which pioneer conditions, now belonging to history, implanted in them and their fathers, and which schools, newspapers, radio and movies have diligently inculcated. This middle-class way of looking at things has been greatly abetted by nationalist and race feeling. In the long procession of unemployed who have come to me with pleas and complaints I have literally heard more outcries against "the boss" for employing only naturalized or unnaturalized Americans, or whites or colored workers, as the case may be, in discrimination against the others, than against the boss as the exponent of a cruel and stupid system.

The writing of this paper was interrupted by a day

at a meeting of the New York City Board of Estimate
and Apportionment at which bus franchises for the
Borough of Queens were considered. The hearing fur-
nished a striking illustration of the slant of the American mind and the things Americans will protest
against. The room was filled with indignant citizens,
overwhelmingly of the wage and salary working class,
who came to protest, not primarily at a bus monopoly
which seemed to offer 112 per cent annual profit to
private monopolists, not to urge non-political city
operation, but to rally around certain independent
operators who were likely to lose a good thing. Granting that some of these operators had deserved fairly
well of the communities served, the individualist
point of view of the protesting delegations gave a
socialist something to think about.

Perhaps the vogue of that clerical demagogue,
Father Coughlin of Detroit, is the best single illustration of my point. His tremendously popular radio
addresses attack indiscriminately heartless employers,
bankers, Henry Ford, internationalists, birth control
advocates, socialists and communists. He came to
New York to eulogize Mayor Walker and berate his
critics at a Communion breakfast of the Holy Name
Society—without any real knowledge of the city situation, but with no lack of fervor in his ignorance. Yet
this is the man with whom I have been told at a work-
ingmen's forum in the Middle West that we all ought
to unite!

Father Coughlin is a Roman Catholic with a hearing among Protestants as well as Catholics probably greater at the moment than any anti-Catholic demogogue. But the Ku Klux spirit among Protestant Nordics is far from dead even if the organization itself is happily no longer very strong.

For these discordant, racial, nationalistic and religious groups in our midst it will not be an easy thing to find a common denominator. Our economic overlords can probably for a time longer utilize these prejudices to enable them to divide and govern. But the way these overlords are floundering in this economic crisis makes it far less probable than it seemed in 1928 that they can indefinitely use the old machinery of propaganda and their control of both old parties to perpetuate and consolidate their power. There is a ruthlessness and suspicion in America, and skeptical disbelief in political action, which, given a few more years of bad economic conditions, will furnish a splendid field for an American Hitler to exploit. Such a fascist leader could not be purely imitative any more than Hitler merely imitated Mussolini. The exact circumstances under which he could get his start I do not venture to predict. What is essential is that he should be colorful enough, resourceful enough in picking prejudices to exploit, nationalistic enough, and apparently radical enough, to appeal to the masses, while at the same time openly or secretly he stands in with enough bankers or industrialists to finance his movement as an alternative to socialism or communism. His scheme will at least have to provide for rudimentary economic planning and unemployment insurance. Hitler illustrates this sort of thing in Germany. Outwardly he represents a kind of last stand of the little man, of the respectable patriotic German who sees his world hopelessly slipping in the post-war confusion and wants to do something about it. But enough big men have confidence in his and their power to manipulate a movement—on the face of it directed against them—to finance it, somewhat as the industrialists of Italy at the proper moment rallied behind the radical Mussolini and so saved—for a time—their beloved profit system.

At this point the gentle and not so gentle reader who has condescended to follow me so far may yearn to make vigorous protest: "America isn't Germany, our democratic tradition is better established, our two-party system is preferable to European multiplicity of parties and less favorable to the rise of fascism." Perhaps; certainly, I repeat, American fascism will have features peculiar to America. Nevertheless my own conviction is that American proneness to violence, American contempt for law as law —witness our racketeers and ponder the fate of the 18th Amendment—and above all the impotence of the old parties in an economic crisis, provide fertile soil for an extra-legal political movement. The present drift of things means that such a movement to gain great strength within a decade will be, broadly speaking, fascist in nature rather than communist. Communism, however, will gain as a factor to be reckoned with, especially if the Russian planned economy is as successful as now seems likely. But for communism to triumph within a decade—short of the debacle of a new world war into which America should be drawn—would require at the least a defeat of all forms of European fascism so dramatic and convincing that it would appear even to the most "patriotic" Americans that the fault was not in some European party or persons, but in the whole ultra-nationalist basis of fascism. If by that defeat dictatorship as well as nationalism is discredited, socialism rather than communism will benefit.

Three events occurring since these pages were first written greatly strengthen my belief in the drift to fascism. One of them was the appearance of the Swope Plan for reorganizing industry into trade associations regulated by the government. This proposal is a complete denial of the bases of the old capitalism, but it sets up instead a capitalist syndicalism still operated for profit, a scheme which in essence is fascist and not socialist. Almost at the time Mr. Swope made public his plan the American Legion adopted a resolution drafted by another captain of industry, Mr. Howard Coffin, for a peacetime Council of Defense with semi-dictatorial powers. By its conduct the Legion suggests that, bribed by a judicious mixture of beer and bonus, it may serve as the equivalent of Mussolini's Black Shirts.

A third event showing a general drift to fascism was the sweeping Tory triumph in the British elections. This was a last flare-up of a dying order which cloaked its greed and folly in an emotional nationalism and won to itself the powerful aid of that tragically mistaken leader, Ramsay MacDonald. The resultant national government takes office without plan or mandate on a blank check to save England. It will rule for a while with a disguised parliamentary dictatorship. This, however, is not likely to endure. Despite British Labor's mistakes, of which the greatest was to cling to office at the price of power, there is more hope for democracy in British labor than in any present organized force in America. The Tory triumph, however, temporarily will assist the American drift to fascism. It marks pretty definitely the decision of capitalism to make its last stand with nationalism rather than going internationalist as some had hoped and others feared. Capitalism needs nationalism to hypnotize the workers whom it exploits.

All this attempted prophecy is postulated on the assumption that we continue to drift. It is also postulated on the assumption that we avoid new world war. What would emerge out of new world war save stark madness and destruction, I do not venture to predict. Such war, probably beginning as a war between nations, would soon be complicated by class revolts and by the rising of colored races in colonies exploited by the white man. This very danger may help to restrain the more powerful nations from war. Fear of internal revolution as well as their mutual jealousies of one another make rather unlikely that organized attack of capitalist nations on Russia which some capitalist chauvinists desire, and orthodox communists think inevitable. On the other hand, Russia's concern for her own development, and the strong sense of realism her rulers have shown in actual diplomatic relations, make Russian attack on capitalist nations within the decade far less likely than alarmists of the Matthew Woll school profess to fear.

But there are plenty of probable occasions for a war into which nations may stumble and blunder. There is the critical situation in Manchuria whose end no man can foresee. The collapse of Germany, which it is not yet certain that President Hoover's belated recognition of economic realities in an interdependent world can avert, may easily precipitate a conflict of which no one can predict anything save that it will be the suicide of our civilization. If that is temporarily averted there is plenty of menace to peace in the armament race. He is surely an optimist who expects an easy solution of the problem at Geneva. Indeed, as one looks over a world torn by the conflict between the political desire for absolute national independence and the economic compulsions of interdependence of nations, one cannot escape the conclusion that world war within the decade is more likely than world peace. Consider, for instance, Sir George Paish's prescription for peace, or at any rate international stability, in his *The Way to Recovery*, with his insistence on international free trade, and reflect how remote now seems its attainment. In the light of these facts Bertrand Russell has apparently accepted the inevitability of another world war but hopes for a sufficient degree of world government to come out of it to guarantee future peace. I doubt the *inevitability* of that world war and still more do I doubt that if it comes it will be the last war. Chaos and dark night seem to me to be more likely than world government to be its consequence.

Thus, whether we look at home or abroad, we come to the same conclusion. Drift is drift to disaster. The possibility of achieving without catastrophe the inevitable revolutionary changes which a machine age imposes on us requires in the United States the assertion of a capacity for working out a program and putting power behind it which does not exist in the old parties or in the present leadership of the A. F. of L. The socialist program points the way, but the socialism that will be our savior must show a power it now sadly lacks in America and which it has shown in less degree than some of us had hoped in the work of the British Labor Party. To say this is not to damn socialism but to plead for more of it. It is not to discourage the workers and their honest sympathizers from joining the great crusade for achieving revolutionary ends by the revolutionary means of substituting other methods of struggle for great-scale violence; it is rather urging them to come into the crusade. If all the men and women who in their hearts accept to-day the essentials of socialism, who know that our hope depends on owning collectively and operating intelligently for use, not profit, the things necessary for our common life, would to-day actively come into the socialist movement, that one act would greatly change the nature of what we may expect within the next decade. It is not fate but ourselves who may make catastrophe inevitable—unless, indeed, one is to believe that fate has imposed upon us a paralysis of will and intelligence so that we cannot learn to control for life and not for death the machines we have had the wit to make, and the powers of nature we have learned to master.

THE ACCEPTANCE OF VIOLENCE

OURS is a generation which reads Remarque, weeps over *Journey's End*, signs a Kellogg pact to outlaw war, knows the deadliness of modern means of destruction, and then with an amazing degree of unanimity accepts large-scale violence as inevitable or in some circumstances almost desirable. It is this psychological attitude, this predisposition to a kind of collective suicide, which makes the future so dark.

This statement may at first arouse dissent. There are certain conventional bits of optimism, essentially false, which by their very respectability and the frequent iteration of them gain an unthinking belief. Among them are the notions that "we Americans are an essentially peaceful people" and one "not prone to violence." As a matter of fact we have been a pioneer people, both lawless and violent in taking what we wanted. We had grievances against both England and France in 1812 but chose war with England largely in hope—disappointed by our military incompetency —of conquering Canada. Our war against Mexico was a pure war of aggression. Our relations with the Indians have been described as "an unbroken record of broken treaties"—treaties broken to the accompaniment of ruthless violence. Domestic violence and certainly lawlessness have attended the growth of most of our great fortunes and of the great corporate mergers. Frequently there has been more violence in an American strike (often begun or instigated by the employer) than in a *coup d'état* in Europe. Violence is the life blood of that racketeering which has been amazingly promoted by the general contempt for the 18th Amendment, but which is by no means simply a product of legislation which the public wished, apparently, to enact, but never truly to enforce. Finally, to our everlasting shame, it must be recorded that we are the only supposedly civilized people who have for generations punctuated our indifferent tolerance of crime with the lurid lawlessness of lynchings. Surely this is not a record to invite other nations or ourselves to accept at anything like their face value our professions of law-abiding peacefulness.

The best that can be said for us is that like most peoples we do not consciously desire war—at any rate, not large-scale war—that we are not deliberately aggressive despite occasional appearances to the contrary, notably in the Caribbean; in short, that on the abstract issue of war or peace the overwhelming majority of us are for peace.

But this is very far from contradicting the truth of that acceptance or expectation of violence which is our present theme. It is an expectation shared by men and women with almost nothing else in common, by men and women who differ vehemently concerning the appropriate object of violence. The D. A. R. and the communists have this faith to make them brothers and sisters under the skin. A majority of the Supreme Court has again affirmed that a willingness to bear arms in any and every war the political state may decree, regardless of one's conscience or religious scruples, is the ultimate test of the right of a man or a woman to be admitted to citizenship. What but an amazing degree of expectation of violence can thus explain a decision which would bar from citizenship, in the nation which fathered the Kellogg Pact, Jesus Christ and William Penn, Einstein and Gandhi, and would give to the state which criticizes Soviet Russia in the name of individual liberty an absolute right to send men to their death in a war in which they do not believe? Certainly nothing else can explain the irrelevance of compulsory military training in the high schools and the universities.

Neither in private talk nor public discussion with any official of our military services have I ever discovered real faith that any conceivable kind or degree of military preparation would of itself guarantee lasting peace. It might, my friends and critics thought, prevent some wars and make victory more likely in the wars from which there will be no escape.

In this matter there is no great variance between military and non-military opinion. I suppose that a popular referendum on war would almost always go against war, but even under different legal machinery than we now have it would be comparatively easy to stampede or manipulate the crowd to those choices which would make war inevitable, referendum or no referendum. In these matters it is not the extension but the intensity of the emotion that counts. Most of the time most people have some slogan or interest or prejudice about which they care far more than about peace. I have even seen this illustrated, amusingly and alarmingly, at peace meetings which obviously cared more for highly controversial issues, then prevailing, like Russian politics or Irish, than about the world peace for which they were called together. The oldest of American peace societies actually boasts that it has supported the government in every war. Certainly preachers who are eloquently for peace in time of peace are even more vehement for war in time of war. Conscientious objectors had a worse time with chaplains and pulpit warriors than with army officers. To be sure, since the war a new note of uncompromising pacifism has come into the utterance of many churchmen. It still remains to be tested.

At any rate, public opinion is far from pacifist. Nor has this situation been altered by the so-called outlawry of war in which even the blind can see that neither governments nor peoples put much faith. Oh, yes; they all mean to keep their pact, but none of them is sure about the others!

It is, however, by no means only in the field of foreign policies and the relation of nations to one another than there is this expectation of violence. There can be no question but that there has been within the last year and a half an enormous growth of conviction in the United States that there can be, or at any rate will be, no fruitful social change save by violent revolution. The men and women who profess this belief very seldom belong to the small Communist Party. Some of them are a rather unadmirable type of parlor reds who take out in talk their social heresies. These men and women, usually intellectuals or at least college graduates, are simply compensating for the futility of their actions by the violence of their opinions. Not all those who accept or expect violence fall under this condemnation. Once after I had delivered an address on this subject at a college I was told that a class which had been reading my book, *America's Way Out: A Program for Democracy*, had decided unanimously that they sympathized with my ends, but that they could only be achieved through violence. Among those workers who take part in forum discussions, there is a pathetic and illogical assurance that capitalism is too strong for the labor unions or a political party of the workers and that *therefore* we must wait for the violent revolution which by some blissful certainty will be the right sort of revolution bound somehow to make the weak wise and strong. Meanwhile these future revolutionists docilely take what they can get from the old-line economic and political bosses.

It is easy to smile at this modern version of the old

apocalyptic hope of persecuted Jews and Christians that the worse things become the nearer is the day of their salvation. It is, however, by no means certain that the exploited who neglect to use effectively the opportunities they now have may not in some moment of crisis, let us say in the misery of new world war, find a strength for violent revolution which now they lack. It is even now significant that the communists in New York and other cities can find more men and women occasionally to demonstrate with them even at the risk of police attack than to vote with them.

The very fact that the acceptance of violence as inevitable to gain or keep desirable social ends is so nearly universal, argues that there must be reasons for it worth examining. Man has always been combative, partly because by fighting he has got or kept what he wanted, partly for love of mastery, but very largely among the rank and file of human beings because of sheer fear. There is an extremity of fear which causes a retreat or a submissiveness which is cringing, resentful but impotent, the last abasement of the human spirit. But short of this extreme, men who are afraid usually plan overt action to make themselves safe. Bertrand Russell in an interesting paragraph declares: "At the present time the fiercest and most dangerous animal with which human beings have to contend is man, and the dangers arising from purely physical causes have been very rapidly reduced.

In the present day, therefore, fear finds little scope except in relation to other human beings, and fear itself is one of the main reasons why human beings are formidable to each other. It is a recognized maxim that the best defense is attack; consequently people are continually attacking each other because they expect to be attacked. Our instinctive emotions are those that we have inherited from a much more dangerous world, and contain, therefore, a larger proportion of fear than they should; this fear, since it finds little outlet elsewhere, directs itself against the social environment, producing distrust and hate, envy, malice, and all uncharitableness."

Nevertheless, war, and especially modern war, is not a simple automatic product of fear. Civic organization within nations, imperfect as it is, has made the appeal to violence exceptional and unusual. Force, to be sure, still persists. Government implies some coercion, but usually it is a comparative non-violent coercion. Police force may often be used excessively, unfairly, and for unjust ends, but it differs greatly from war. It is not, like the violence of war, anarchistic, indiscriminate, uncontrolled, and directed to wholesale destruction. Yet the workers of any country have more reason for fearing and hating their domestic exploiters than their fellow-workers in foreign lands. Only the existing international anarchy, the absolute claims of rival states and the hypnotic power of nationalism, make it possible for the collective group fears, hates and greeds of nations to result in war. So far are fear and hate of soldiers in rival armies from being "natural" or "instinctive" that in the great World War they were kept alive among soldiers and civilians only by constant propaganda.

Moreover, modern war for civilians, and even for combatants, involves hideous risks without the emotional relief and excitement of hand-to-hand conflict. Under these circumstances, war, or rather the possibility of war, is psychologically anything but a simple product of fear or hate or combativeness. The acceptance of the violence of war is only possible because of the long tradition of war and the inculcation of a patriotism, from the cradle to the grave, which is consciously identified with military success. That war has been a habit cannot be denied. In 1894 the *Moscow Gazette* listed 286 wars in Europe alone in the preceding three centuries—an average of almost one a year. It is hard to struggle against such a habit, but not hopeless.

War as a social institution had a definite beginning in human experience; it may have an end. There was a reason for war when tribes fought for limited areas of fertile land which is lacking when the same science which makes war so incredibly deadly makes it possible in a properly organized world to end poverty for everybody.

The case against acceptance of the violence of war is overwhelming. We lived through the ghastly, grisly years from 1914 to 1918, lured by visions more false than any mirage on the burning desert. The war cost 30 million lives, soldiers and civilians, and some 340 billion dollars. It left a legacy of broken men and women, ill nourished children, all ripe for perpetuating endless fear and hate. It did not end war, make the world safe for democracy, vindicate forever the rights of small nations, or give a new soul to men. Not a single one of the idealist hopes wherewith the war was gilded for the suffering nations has been fulfilled. Not even the most ardent admirer of the League of Nations can pretend that its hesitant advances in internationalism have been worth one small part of the unutterable misery of front-line trench and refugee camp. Every great nation engaged, except Russia, is to-day definitely the worse for the struggle, and the Russian revolution was made by men who hated the war and was violently opposed by both sets of belligerents. There is not the slightest reason to think that in terms of results the history of any future world war will be different. Modern war is loss and only loss for every combatant. In every succeeding world war it will be more true than in the one that has gone before that there will be no victors, but only survivors, who may in the agony of what they have endured envy the dead who sleep.

It is a social asset of real importance that we have so many veracious and moving accounts of the last war; of its shoddy lies and hypocrisies and propaganda; of the mud and vermin of its trenches; of the indiscriminate and indescribable horror and cruelty of its carnage. The good militarist and imperialist, Winston Churchill, in a picturesque passage deplores the degeneracy of war from its status as a beautiful game to a thing of sordid misery at the hands of democracy and science.

It is probable that no picture of the war of 1914-1918 in any language will be adequate to the terrors of new world war. That will be war in which there can be no non-combatants. Women and children are the inevitable victims of warriors of the air and cities the necessary goal of the destruction they will rain down from the very heavens to which men have reached up hands for blessing. The expert reports at the Brussels Conference of the International Red Cross were unanimous in saying that against chemical warfare from the air there can be no protection. And it is wholly probable that nations mad enough to go to war will not stop with chemicals but will use bacteria and lethal rays to destroy the enemy—men, women and children alike.

To make headway against acceptance of the violence of international war is, then, in the first instance, a matter of education in the deadliness and self-defeating nature of modern war. That education cannot dwell too much on horror. A thoughtful high school teacher tells me that he thinks he is achieving results by reading to boys still believing in the romance of war, stories of the last war. Probably he is right. Yet possibly these stories may have a strange compulsion to a generation avid for new sensations and sensitive to the comradeship in suffering which some war stories reveal.

Whether this is true or not, it is certainly true that we shall not be saved merely by new fears for old. Fear is as often mother of panic as of wisdom. It is already obvious that mere realization of the deadliness of war will not automatically save us. Rather it still makes for the old, old ways of folly, for that military preparation which, as General Maurice has reminded us, tends to get us that for which we prepare. It is one of the besetting sins of many peace lovers that they think mere denunciation of war and violence is enough.

Obviously we who believe that the acceptance of the violence of new world war is virtual suicide must seek substitutes both for the international anarchy and injustice and the false education in nationalism which give occasion to war. We cannot fall into the delusion that in our sort of world our favorite patent medicine on the drug store shelves will give us peace. Disarmament, removal of economic barriers, arbitration, world courts, these and other devices have their uses. No one of them can stand alone as the sole way to peace.

This is not the place to outline a complete program for world peace, but it would be a very academic performance in times of tension like ours to deplore the acceptance of violence and yet to keep silence on the overwhelming importance to peace of such immediate measures as cleaning the slate of the tangle of German reparations and inter-Allied debts, the recognition of Russia by the United States with an end to the folly of boycotts and embargoes or the discussion of them, and the success of all efforts for disarmaments. These are only the first steps in a program of organizing the economy of an interdependent world, its trade and its fiscal system as befits a brotherhood of workers' republics.

These are political measures requiring collective action. The individual as citizen should do all he can to further them. There are other things the individual can do very directly. Dr. Einstein has said that if two per cent of the young men of any country would let it be known that under no circumstances would they voluntarily or under conscription engage in new war between the nations, but would instead fill the jails, the statesmen would find a way to avoid war. This statement (which would make Dr. Einstein ineligible to citizenship in the nation whose principal city through none other than the Honorable Jimmy Walker gave him its key) is very suggestive. Whether the exact per cent is two or more, certainly the growth of a convinced and determined group of objectors to war who mean business is a tremendously useful antidote to the unthinking acceptance of violence.

One of the most powerful of possible preventives of war would be a general strike against an impending war by organized workers. This would be an example of the use of non-violent coercion against violence; and the development of means of non-violent coercion is of revolutionary significance.

The need of non-violent means of coercing the exploiter or of struggling against injustice is of particular importance when we examine the reasons for violence on the part of the workers. It is untrue to say that "violence never works." It may be terribly costly, but it has got results. In moderate doses, as Louis Adamic has said, it has been publicity for the under dog. It also serves as warning that he may have power. Slaves content to be slaves, workers content to starve quietly, never get deliverance from heaven or from sheer human kindness. And the natural vehicle of their protest, especially given our Western traditions (quite unlike the Indian tradition to which Gandhi has appealed), is some degree of violence. No honest and intelligent person can say that in our imperfect democracy we have a polite and easy substitute for violence in the right to organize unions and to vote. The most we can say is that there is a power in it not adequately asserted by the workers of America. Ballots are better than bullets and an organized strike than a riot. The history of such considerable labor violence as was used by the Molly Maguires, the Pittsburgh and Baltimore rioters of the seventies, and the dynamiters in Los Angeles, is a history of a great setback for labor. It was not altogether useful publicity for the under dog! Yet he lacks imagination who does not see why the harassed worker or striker, seeing his job taken and his struggle defeated by a scab under police protection, finding himself evicted, perhaps at night from his home, takes to himself a stone, a club or a gun rather than a ballot. No exploited class can afford to let the masters think it will not use violence unless it can discover a more effective instrument of struggle than violence.

In the shocking lack of public provision for the economic misery of this winter our upper class has given supreme evidence of a callous heartlessness which invites riots and will make those who suffer in them martyrs of the working class.

It is true that the record of labor violence in American labor struggles on both sides is grim, yet Mr. Adamic would have given a fairer picture in *Dynamite* if he had pointed out that the whole labor struggle in England and America since the beginning of the industrial revolution, a struggle against the most abominable exploitation, has thus far been carried on with only a tithe of the violence which marked a single day when all was quiet on the western front. It is the glory of the labor movement that it has gone as far as it has in perfecting a comparatively non-violent means of struggling for justice by the strike. Hope lies in developing such means of resistance. For the workers merely to renounce violence with no substitute in sight would be to play into the hands of the oppressor.

Our present concern is not with the occasional and almost incidental use of violence but with the acceptance of it as *necessary* for revolutionary ends. Here we face not only, it is alleged, lack of a substitute for violence, but a positive advantage in the drama and ruthlessness of the final act of violence at the revolutionary moment. It is true that sometimes old-fashioned revolution cleared the way for action, burned up much rubbish, and ended the paralysis of the will which tends to defeat even the most moderate change under the old order. Consider how many abuses and annoyances we put up with in America now—like, for instance, the lame duck session of Congress— which no one, save a few politicians, wants at all. These admissions can be expanded and embroidered to the heart's content of the most violent revolutionary and it will still remain true that there is no certainty that in the fires of revolution only hay and stubble, the dross and dirt of life, will be burned. Some very precious liberties and ancient sanctions of individual right will go also. And some evil legacies of hate will be left. It is the tragedy of history that lovers of liberty and justice have always blunted the edge of their own idealism, sown the seeds of new oppressions, debased the shining cities of their dreams by the wholesale violence they have felt obliged to use.

But this calm acceptance of revolutionary violence at the price of doing some of the immediate things that might make it unnecessary springs mostly not from the facts but from certain misconceptions of the past and the present.

Even in the bloody pages of human history not all struggle has meant war. There has been no relation whatever between the proportion of violence and the proportion of social achievement. The lurid lights of the French revolution have blinded men. I shall not argue, as I might, that some of its violence was more accidental and incidental, more rooted in the crimes and blunders of particular men than immutably de-creed as the birth pangs of a new order of society. Rather let me point out once more that some of the cruelest wars in history have been dynastic or per-sonal, almost without social significance, while pro-found changes in human institutions and the distribu-tion of property and power have been attended with little or no violence. If the struggle for the emanci-pation of women is not wholly analogous to class or national struggle, it is at least significant that chattel slavery was abolished in every country but the United States without violence, and that the shift from feu-dalism to capitalism was accomplished in England without internal violence after the Cromwellian wars, and in Japan within scarcely more than a generation with only a trifling revolt.

It is too early to hold up Spain as an example of successful and almost wholly non-violent *social* revolution. It has given an example of how determined and well organized workers can make a *political* revolution without violence. If kings or their economic counterparts have to do their own fighting, there will be few wars!

If history is not wholly on the side of inevitable violence, neither is a common-sense view of existing conditions. The resources of science for destruction can be as well applied to civil as to foreign war. The barricade is a futile and archaic symbol of revolution against a government which can keep the loyalty of its air squadrons. From the air was popular revolution in Cuba defeated and the mutiny of the Chilean navy conquered. If a government cannot keep the loyalty of the air forces there need be no barricades. The very complexity of the processes for feeding the industrial masses is another reason why the headlong appeal to a violence which may cut off water and milk and food will be self-defeating.

The moral of this is twofold. It applies to two opposite groups. It is, first of all, a moral for those whose acceptance of violence makes them hold aloof from, or sneer at, the effort to produce results by

political organization and action. Such action if successful may make your violent revolution unnecessary; if not, it is likely greatly to reduce the resistance
that will be offered to workers used to acting together.
It is a thousand times worth trying. Nor are we who
want to try these orderly and legal ways of serving
labor's cause eternally wedded to legalism. We want
to escape the onus of seeking violence, an onus
which has done immense harm to American radicalism among the very people it would serve. We want
to put the onus of love of violence where it rightly
belongs: on those who scruple at no trickery or force
to hold the unjust power and privilege they have.
But the weapons of non-violent revolutionaries will
not always be wholly and solely legal. Under conditions that make it necessary they will seek ways to
interpret and apply in the West those methods of
demonstration and non-violent coöperation which
Gandhi has thus far employed with amazing success
in the Indian revolution. There are times when honest
men must explain why they are not in jail, and when
a willingness to endure without flinching is more effective than the will to fight. The final and most difficult revolution will not be in the ends men seek but
in the means they use. To cling blindly to violence
is in our day close to a reactionary counsel of despair.

But—and here is the second part of this moral—
the responsibility for violence is never chiefly on those
who rise at last against oppression. It is rather on

those whose selfishness, apathy and stupidity, make them stand unyieldingly for their privileges at no matter what cost of violence—usually vicarious! There are well-meaning folks who talk almost like Tolstoians when labor is accused of violence, who will not understand that they are themselves the beneficiaries of the latent or actual violence of the unjust social order against which long exploited classes and races some day will rebel. The critic of labor or revolutionary violence is an arrant hypocrite unless he does all that in him lies to open those paths of free, non-violent progress on which our hope depends!

How great is that hope? Each month of drift makes it less. But still the cost of the acceptance of violence in the age of airplanes and poison gas is so great that we shall not forgive ourselves nor will our children forgive us if we do not seek a more excellent way.

History is written by survivors, and some survivors there will be from the series of violent struggles toward which we drift. In some far distant future these survivors may complacently boast of gains out of these losses which now we contemplate. But to our generation who must endure and suffer, go mad with hate and fear and lust of blood, the possible optimism of future historians can have no meaning. If we are to endure for any reason whatsoever this anguish of suffering, this madness of hate and destruction, better for us by far that we had never known the beauty, the hopes, the dreams, the friendships by which alone we live. What have we to do with hopes and dreams and remembered delights who are predestined cannon fodder, foredoomed victims of the destruction that will fall on us from the skies and rise to overwhelm us from the earth? It is because such violence will be the destruction at least of a generation that its easy acceptance is an enemy to be fought without quarter as we hope for life.

DISARMAMENT AND PEACE

THERE is, on the whole, a gratifying growth of sentiment for disarmament in the United States. Not only is there interest in international conference on disarmament but in American leadership in disarmament. So conservative a politician as President Hoover solemnly warned the European nations (rather than ourselves) on the eve of our showy air maneuvers, that the burden of armaments, costing the nations $5,000,000,000 a year, is *the* cause of world depression. In passing, one may applaud the President's concern about the economic burden of armaments while denying that it is the cause of a world depression rooted in our chaotic unplanned profit system and accentuated by our various nationalist follies of which competitive armaments are one. Russia and France have felt the depression least of great nations although they are among the most heavily armed.

But the new American interest in the general problem of armaments does not of itself guarantee wise leadership toward peace. Japan produced one million signatures to a petition for drastic disarmament only a little while before her militarists began intervention in Manchuria. Advocacy of disarmament is by no means the sole and sufficient road to peace. Nations which think only in terms of physical disarmament will not disarm, and if by some miracle they should, they would still be able to carry on the most deadly form of modern warfare. Any strong nation, well equipped in chemical industry and airplanes, can improvise the kind of war which will lay a whole countryside waste and make the glory of great cities one with Nineveh and Tyre. On the whole the United States would gain, not lose, in this sort of disarmament. If later on war should come, our geographic and industrial position would give us an immense advantage in a war of the air for which no nation was directly prepared. Let some of our idealists remember this before they feel too noble, and our militarists before they shed too many tears for the fate of America in a disarmed world!

With these words of caution against claiming too much, let us see the immense strength of the rational argument for the value of disarmament.

In the first place, a poverty-stricken world is close to madness when it spends the huge sum of $5,000,-000,000 and takes millions of young men out of useful work, for something that is in itself wholly unproductive, satisfies no reasonable want or need of men, and does not, as innumerable wars testify, serve as good insurance against disaster. Everyone interested in ending illiteracy, demolishing slums, eradicating plagues like hook worm or pellagra, gnashes his teeth when he considers the cost of one battleship or cruiser. It is unquestionably true that economic conditions over much of Europe are worse than before the World War, partly because the dubious blessing of national independence for many of the smaller states has meant a great increase in their military burdens, the costs of which have come out of the incomes of already poor peasants who bear the additional burden of absurdly high tariffs due also to a false nationalistic pride. To this extent has armament contributed to world depression.

Nevertheless, suddenly to abandon armaments would not of itself immediately and automatically end depression. It might rather temporarily add to the number of the unemployed. It would be necessary to have some plan for a better use of the national income, some scheme for helping the military personnel to fit into productive labor.

In the second place, while disarmament alone and of itself will not prevent war, it will make it far less likely. For this there are several outstanding reasons:

1. Armaments mean a military caste; a military caste is bound by the nature of its training and the logic of its profession to accept the philosophy of militarism, to work steadily for more armaments—did any General Staff ever regard any degree of preparedness as adequate?—and even sometimes to encourage the coming of war itself. Let me hasten to add that this is not to accuse military men of being essentially bloodthirsty or consciously insincere in their professed love of peace. In America our com-

paratively small military caste has heretofore had less to do with getting us into war than economic interest and the propaganda of such a jingoistic press as was largely responsible for our inglorious and wholly unnecessary Spanish war.

In Europe the rôle of the military has been more sinister. Even in our own country it is impossible to explain the zeal of the War Department and army officers for compulsory military training in high schools and colleges in any other terms than their desire to inoculate as many of our citizens as possible with the philosophy of militarism, a philosophy which, as their own manuals show, is essentially undemocratic. No rational man, soldier or civilian, believes that the kind of drill we have on our college campuses is the best form of physical training, makes character or, what is more to the point, really trains soldiers. The unpleasant parts of training soldiers, like bayonet drill, are left out to please the mothers. Drill is prettified with honorary girl colonels and sugared over by the offer of the use of polo ponies. But popular or unpopular, it may induce young men to accept the point of view of the Pharaohs on national protection. Already it has helped to give us a reserve officers' association which lobbies powerfully for military appropriations.

So far as professional officers are concerned, it would be at least as strange were they never to want to try out their knowledge as for a surgeon to hope for the end of all operations. They cannot try out their profession even on paper without a theoretical enemy and that theoretical enemy cannot be the moon or Mars. Hence plans for war against this nation or that with a gradual growth of the appropriate psychology. I have rarely discussed this question with an army or navy man publicly or privately without discovering that he had a definite foe in mind. Ten years ago it was Japan, three years ago it was England; to-day Brigadier General Lucius R. Holbrook tells a reunion of the 78th Division—and the world—that the enemy will be Russia with Germany as an ally. Meanwhile most books by World War generals tell us how we suffered from lack of more and earlier preparation—an argument which has rather less than no weight with those of us who believe that we and the world would have been infinitely better off if we had kept out of Europe's war of rival imperialisms.

2. A second boon of disarmament would be that it would remove or greatly lessen the rich financial prize for which armament makers strive. The part which armament makers played prior to the World War in keeping alive the intrigues and fomenting the state of mind out of which wars came has been often discussed. Everybody knows that Turks killed British soldiers at Gallipoli with British guns. Since the Great War less has been said about the international armament ring. I do not profess to know what armament makers do to help make the demand for the things they supply. It

has been very large in China, Latin America and Europe. The business of selling guns to whomever has the price ranks with the narcotic trade in infamy. Even if armament making were nationalized to remove private profit there would still be the interest of steel makers and others in selling material for armaments. We would still have "big drum" Shearers financed by interested parties to discredit conferences or armaments. The best way is go to the farthest possible limit in getting rid of the business once and for all.

3. An even weightier argument for disarmament is the fact that while disarmed nations can improvise means, and deadly means of warfare, they cannot do it without some delay during which sober second thought may get in its work. I have never been able to read any account of the origins of the World War without an overwhelming conviction that if Austria, Russia, Germany and France could not have mobilized in twenty-four hours the war might have been avoided. Disarmed nations will be harder for militarists, profiteers, newspapers and stupid diplomats to stampede into great war.

4. Weightiest of all the arguments for disarmament is the fact that no nation ever has supported, ever will or even can support, the enormous burden of armament against war in general or against an abstract and indefinite danger. Nations, as Senor De Madariaga

has well put it, do not arm against war but against a war. England has maintained her navy in the last two centuries first with an eye on France, then Russia, then Germany, and now the United States and France. So with other nations and their military leaders, including, as I have previously remarked, our own retired but untired rear admirals. Thus in the act of maintaining armaments for protection each nation automatically increases the fear and suspicion of some other nation out of which war is born. Even though, as I firmly believe, the main root of war is economic rivalry of nations, that root could not easily put forth so evil a tree of destruction were it not nourished in this soil of suspicion. To keep competitive armaments alive requires the maintenance and increase of suspicion.

There is not a single nation in the world that professes desire to conquer its neighbors. Every nation professes to-day, even after signing the Kellogg Pact, that it arms only for defense. It is inconceivable that the mass of workers could be led to face war on any other count. Certainly only a belief that each people fought for the fatherland made the World War possible. Against the insecurity of armament which that war so tragically illustrated have been the security and peace of Canada and the United States with 3,000 miles of undefended boundary. It is only the hideous complex of suspicion, fear and hate which keeps alive the burden of armament, and the chief result of that burden is to heighten the suspicion which gave it birth.

It is idle to talk about armaments as insurance, not only for the reasons we have discussed, but for the final and conclusive reason that in our world no nation, not even our own, is strong enough to achieve superiority in arms against every conceivable combination of enemies that can be brought against it. The attempt to do anything of the sort augments the zeal for forming alliances and counter-alliances and increases the likelihood of the formation, out of sheer fear and suspicion, of a union strong enough to defeat the nation which proudly seeks military superiority.

There is a domestic aspect of this question that deserves more attention from peace lovers than it has had. It is that the growing ease with which certain branches of the armed services, notably the air force, can be turned against civilians and made into a modern equivalent of the ancient pretorian guard. In recent months Machado suppressed a revolution in Cuba, despite the general hatred of him, primarily because his small but well paid air force was loyal; then the air force saved the Chilian government from naval mutiny. Even in Great Britain, the mother of parliaments, had to make quicker terms with a navy angry over drastic wage cuts than with civilians. Now these services, so easily capable of becoming the modern pretorian guards, are only supported by civilian tax-payers, at least in quasi-democractic countries, in the name of protection against foreign danger. Thus can fear of the foreign enemy and the current brand of patriotism be turned to the service of the possible tyrants at home.

All the logic, then, is on the side of disarmament. And when I say disarmament I mean disarmament, not a budgetary cut of 25 per cent or 50 per cent, not the abolition of certain classes of fighting machines: battleships, submarines and armed airplanes, for instance. Certainly I do not mean that impossible thing called parity which has produced so much extraordinary mathematics and given such severe headaches to so many of our experts. The easiest parity is the parity of zero. It will not make all nations equal in potential military strength, but nothing will accomplish that miracle. If I want to make a disarmament pact with my next-door neighbors I say: "Let us throw away our guns and keep no convenient rock piles for ammunition." I don't try to figure the number of stones or the calibre of guns our respective heights and weights entitle us to keep. The soundest proposal on disarmament was the Russian. If it was a bluff, it was a bluff worth calling. That it was not called suggests what we all know: there is far more than this simple logic of our general wellbeing to complicate the problem of disarmament.

Armaments, standing armies, great navies, universal conscription of young men: these are but phases

of the general insanity of a world which machinery
has made interdependent but in which the highest
loyalty is to absolute nationalist states which are in
sharp economic competition. This ruthless and usually stupid competition takes place in a world with an
ancient tradition of armament and war, a habit of
accepting violence, a bitter experience of national insecurity, and a tenacious memory of the sins of its
neighbors which each nation deliberately fosters in
its elementary schools and popular books. We have
competitive armaments because we have no real international society, no true family of nations, and because we have competitive armaments it is harder to
get a true family of nations. There is the vicious cir-
cle, and the problem of true statesmanship is where to
take hold of it.

Among the least of the givers to achieve a community of nations may be our own United States. We
are not essentially ungenerous; we are no Uncle Shy-
lock. But for historical reasons that are easily understood we are still eager for a political isolation that our
economic commitments make impossible. We have
not even grasped the elementary fact that if we cannot and will not crush Russia—and we can't—we
must get along with Russia. We alone of the great
nations have not recognized Russia and strong groups
in America talk a world boycott on Russia in defiance
of all common sense. We are even more obstinate
about not facing plain facts of the cost to us and all

nations of a futile attempt to collect debts and reparations.

In other words, of the three steps most immediately necessary for world peace: recognition of, and trade with, Russia, the cancellation of debts and reparations, and the success of the Geneva Conference on Disarmament—three things closely interrelated—it is highly uncertain that either government or people in the United States are ready to take the first two. Indeed it is not certain how far we are ready to go on disarmament, especially in view of our record of insisting on keeping battleships even if Admiral Sims did say that in the next war they would have to go up the Mississippi for shelter. If to the three immediate steps necessary for world recovery we add the fourth of tariff reduction, the rôle of the United States as leader in the cause of peace is much more dubious.

Nevertheless, so far as disarmament goes, the United States is not the chief stumbling block. Perhaps the chief danger to disarmament and to peace is, as I write, Japan's military adventure in Manchuria which has not yet yielded to pressure from the League of Nations or the United States. In the western world the chief obstacle to disarmament is France.

Yet France will hear nothing of disarmament save after the achievement of security. And security apparently requires a world agreement to come with military force to the aid of the victim of aggression.

Well, why not take hold of our problem at this

with armament and the harder to get international organization. The first step in a pioneer community in ending a feud is to get men to lay down their arms; then they can think more clearly about the terms of security. Disarmament, as Arthur Henderson and others have argued eloquently, is the first, not the last, step in security.

The French think otherwise for reasons as easy to understand as some of our own American attitudes which endanger world peace. They, no more than we, are sinners above all others.

On the negative side their attitude is to be explained by a fear of what invasion means, born of bitter memories. On the positive side is the fact that in nationalistic terms France has about what she wants. She merely wants to keep it. With her Slavic allies she is vitally concerned for the preservation of the present boundaries of Europe. Economically she is more nearly self-contained than Great Britain or the United States and has less to fear—though more than some of her spokesmen seem to think—from mere economic collapse in Germany.

Now as Mr. Frank Simonds made appallingly clear at the 1931 Williamstown Institute, the purely nationalist interests of France and her allies in regard to the Polish Corridor, German parity in arms, or German union with Austria, cannot be reconciled with Germany's desires. The conflict in interest goes on now more or less relentlessly even under guise of peace. French guns and gold dominate Europe as never before since the first Napoleon. Premier Laval's visit to President Hoover seems to have been in substance a polite way of emphasizing French hegemony in Europe.

If this were all there was to the story, if ours were a static world, the outlook would be hopeless for disarmament or peace. But just as new forces and interests coming to the surface of men's desires and thinking in the seventeenth century made an end of religious wars which on their own terms were insoluble, so new forces of economic sanity and international coöperation may relieve national tension by making it less important.

Of this even now there are signs, ranging from the partial internationalism of certain capitalist interests (not of themselves likely to bring world peace) to the internationalism of a communism which would submerge every conflict in a universal class war. A more peaceful internationalism found expression in the fraternization of French and German workers at the Vienna Conference of the Socialist International. Already these forces are so strong that no nation can invite war without inviting revolution. Some of these find expression in the work of an imperfect but by no means useless League of Nations. To strengthen international authority based on a loyalty to humanity is the true road to peace. This will be easier in a disarmed world, freed from the economic and psychological handicap of reparations and interallied debt.

Yet whatever the explanation of the French attitude, it is not the Soviet government with its dogmatic expectation of inevitable war, not imperial Britain, not the swashbuckling tyrant Mussolini, but republican France which most imperils the rescue of Germany from disaster and threatens the failure of the Geneva Conference. Either of these calamities and certainly both combined, could make the struggle for world peace, to say nothing of world prosperity, all but hopeless. It becomes the prime concern, then, of world statesmanship to present to Geneva such agreement on disarmament among the nations as to force upon France—if worse comes to worst—the unenviable rôle of standing out against the judgment and conscience of mankind.

Logically the case is overwhelmingly complete for total disarmament save for the forces necessary for internal order. Practically we probably can expect agreement only on a budgetary cut and the abolition of certain of the most dangerous or costly weapons and instruments of warfare. I wish I could add that we might expect abolition of conscription for war. No single thing does more to perpetuate the idea of the irresponsible god-state or the militarist philosophy. As a socialist I believe in a wider use of the state as the trustee of the workers in the economic collectivism forced on us by machinery. I do not believe in it as the rightful lord of conscience and life for the business of setting its choicest youth to kill their comrades of other lands. It is a terrifying thing to find so keen a social thinker as Professor Charles A. Beard in the midst of thought-provoking proposals for a planned economy in America, suggesting that if Europe does not disarm we should come to universal military training and service for defense. Given our relative security by virtue of our geographical position, our economic power, and the divisions among our probable enemies, we need no such defense. Our economic interests, if we cling to capitalist nationalism, now point us on the road to empire. Add the inevitable militarism of universal service, and nothing would keep us from marching along that ancient road of pomp and power, the end of which is doom. Yet this increasing militarization of America may well prove a consequence of failure in international reduction of armaments.

Bad as is the outlook, Geneva is not yet a lost battle for peace. The United States has in the war debts a tangible something to offer to a Europe which will not use what we forgive to pay for its competitive arms. The relation of debts and reparations and progress toward disarment is inescapable. The situation calls for an American handling of it, at once enlightened, firm and yet not arrogant. France herself may come to see light. Her relative prosperity is no more immortal than was our own. Despite her self-sufficiency already her trade has dropped, her stock markets have been shaken. Germany may not save herself, but Germany is the Samson who can pull down the pillars of the world order, economic and political, on the heads of all of us, enemies and friends alike.

Today the primary duty of each nation is first to cast out the beam from its own eye. Even if complete international agreement fails at Geneva, even if France holds out for arms, America can well afford an example in disarmament with which other nations and ultimately France would associate themselves. Here I am entirely in agreement with former Ambassador Houghton's stand expressed in his Armistice Day address in New York.

The success, even the partial success, of Geneva will be a good beginning. It will not be the end. The community of nations is still to be achieved and that means more than disarmament. Indeed, it means so much, and our progress toward it is sometimes so slow, that one is tempted to cry out: "Let the old order commit suicide. Let Samson pull down upon us the temple in which by such cruel rites we have worshipped such false gods. Let the Red sword cut the Gordian knots the statesmen could not or would not untie."

But that mood passes when one reflects not only on the price to liberty communism imposes, but on the certainty that the revolt of Germany, probably at the hands in the first instance of Hitlerites, does not mean the establishment in Europe within any short period of so comparatively satisfactory a government and social order as are emerging in Russia, but rather a generation of confused struggle for the mastery between all sorts of men and ideas in the atmosphere of horror that scientific slaughter will create. The new order, the socialism that will save mankind, should be the alternative to world war, not its consequence. Disarmament or progress to disarmament, I repeat, is only a small beginning in the winning of plenty, peace and freedom; it is an important beginning, and if we let it fail it will be the greatest miracle of time if we and our children escape such catastrophe as the world has not yet endured.

would be taxed and stripped of power to the point of elimination.

Yet even Mr. Beard does not bring into the forefront of thinking the essential question of purpose. He leans over backward to prove the native, non-Russian origin of planning in general, and the consistency of his own very advanced proposals with American customs and traditions. Most of the other plans avowedly are directed to salvaging capitalism, profits and all. And some of them are not plans at all but incantations.

The most important of all proposed plans for the simple reason that it comes from one of our authentic captains of industry is Mr. Gerard Swope's plan for a kind of capitalist syndicalism, a stabilization of industry by trade associations subject to federal regulation. Elsewhere in this book I have suggested that this plan looks to an American Fascism. It cuts the ground from under the older competitive capitalism as completely as socialism. But it is vitally concerned still to preserve private property for power and private profit. It ignores, therefore, all questions of landlordism, market speculation and the relation of the profit system, no matter how well stabilized, to cyclical depression. It is not an adequate plan, it is not a popular plan even with business, and to the degree that it might work for a time it would give us a certain stability at the price not only of true prosperity and reasonable economic equality but of liberty. It is a sadly belated effort of the new capitalism to save itself.

Nevertheless this eagerness of a world, that starves because it has produced so much, to find some plan by which to use the machinery it has had the wit to make, is of itself an immensely important sign of the times. It was the essence and the strength of the older economics that it taught faith in automatic processes and laws. Let each man intelligently seek his own good and the ever blessed laws of supply and demand would take care of the rest. Competition assured not only the survival of the strongest but guaranteed that the strongest would be the fittest and the most worthy to survive. Competition—not economic plan—was the guarantor of the general good.

Naturally enough such faith fitted into, and found confirmation from, the prevailing religious beliefs.

Years ago in an old library I came across a little book on theism dating from the early nineteenth century which soberly advanced as one of the soundest arguments for the existence of God the fact that when every man sought his own good the good of all was advanced.

Who but an omnipotent God could arrange matters as nicely as that? Now behold the change. In the very citadels of capitalism, in complete disregard of the assumed efficacy of automatic economic processes, men talk plan.

Nor is it only in the ranks of the capitalists that this great change has occurred. Suppose pre-war anarchists, syndicalists or even most socialists, had been told that by 1931 the great achievement of a communist revolution would have been a five year plan, not evolved spontaneously by emancipated peasants and workers, but imposed on them from on top by an iron discipline which resorted to the piece work and speed-up system, made labor unions the creatures of the dictatorship, and reduced nominal workers' control in factories to a shadow—would it not have been a vast and unwelcome surprise to men who had been proclaiming that all that was really necessary was to break the yoke of capitalism and destroy the profit system and set the workers free? Logically in socialism the notion of planning, especially during a transition period, was always implicit. But it certainly assumed no such commanding place in radical thinking as it has assumed to-day in Russia, and as it must assume if ever power-driven machinery is to be our salvation and not our destruction.

Perhaps the greatest triumph of the Russian dictatorship to date is this: it has taught the lesson that has been implicit in the specialization and interdependence of the machine age—plan or perish. And this lesson has been tragically emphasized for the western world by a degree of economic insecurity, hunger and actual starvation which we are solemnly told is due to overproduction under our hit-or-miss system.

Now of the necessity of planning no one is more fully persuaded than I. But most talk of planning in our capitalist world leaves me a bit cold and skeptical. Some of this talk of planning is consciously or subconsciously presented as a vague but glorious hope of an earthly heaven to dull the discontent of workers in the present hell of unemployment. It rarely takes account of the immediate emergency. It almost always ducks the questions: for whom are we planning, investors, speculators or workers? Are their interests identical, and if so, how far? To men in earnest, the first step in curing our sick society is not plan but purpose. The truly revolutionary decision concerns not the kind of planning commission we shall set up to harness the "billion wild horses" of a machine age, but whether we seriously intend that they shall work for the use of workers rather than the profit of private owners. The Russian revolution preceded the Five Year Plan. And while I profoundly hope that we may learn from Russian experience without repeating it in all its details, we cannot possibly beg the question of socialism versus capitalism by appointing a planning commission. That is several degrees worse than the utopian hope of a "scientific" tariff to be devised by a commission irrespective of determining the previous questions,

why a tariff, what sort of a tariff, and for whose
benefit. A commission on planning may have to
compromise on tactics and next steps; it cannot get
far and compromise on principles. Principle or
philosophy underlies plan.

Stuart Chase, writing on a Ten Year Plan for
America in *Harper's Magazine,* has vividly reminded
us of the success with which we went in for planning in war days. He may be right that physically
the task of peace planning is easier because it concerns only raising the standard of living, while war
planning added to that feeding the maw of the in-
satiable monster, war itself. But he omits or mini-
mizes two considerations:

1. Economically, war planning did little or nothing to interfere with time-honored methods of
financing—liberty loans, etc.—or with profits; witness the 25 per cent average profits of steel com-
panies. These profits did not break down planning
while the war was on because War ever cried for
more. The crisis inherent in the diversion of profit
was postponed to post-war deflations. The economic
set-up for successful peace planning must be very
different and cannot allow for an orgy of high profits,
even with rising wages, if we want to escape recur-
ring crises.

2. Psychologically, the compulsions of war were
understood and had traditionally a force that the
compulsions of unemployment under a capitalist

regime decidedly lack. Even so, notwithstanding the
war compulsions and the tradition of discipline for
war, the indecent haste with which the planning Mr.
Chase praises was scrapped when the Armistice was
signed, shows how alien was planning to the spirit
of capitalism. It will take a terror not yet inspired
by too docile workers to force on capitalism such a
degree of planning as will begin to approximate the
wartime experiment.

But may not the growing concentration of power
to which Mr. Gardiner C. Means calls attention alter
some of the factors? May we not expect some general planning from "the less than 2000" directors of
the 200 largest non-financial corporations which in
1927, according to Mr. Means, controlled "over 45
per cent of the assets of all non-financial corporations, received over 40 per cent of corporate income,
controlled over 35 per cent of all business wealth,
and between 15 and 25 per cent of national wealth"?
The *New Republic*, which editorially is somewhat
optimistic on this point, is candid enough to admit
some of the difficulties. And to its list others can be
added. Great as is the control of these corporations
it does not extend to such vital matters as farming,
bituminous coal mining, building and textiles. There
is little evidence that these 200 great corporations
have tackled or desire to tackle the general economic
problem. Mr. Swope's plan has not met with the
universal applause of his fellow industrialists. The

most the best of them has done is to make some beginning of stabilization within their own industries.
Stabilization of employment has its merits, but the
plain truth is that its general adoption at the present
level of economic activity and at the present rate of
technological advance threatens us with the creation
of a standing army of the permanently unemployed.
All these great corporations shared in the general
speculative debauch; they are dominated by the
prevalent acquisitive and competitive temperament.
They exist to make profits, and production for profit
inevitably means a greater or less degree of both
technological and cyclical unemployment. Why, for
instance, are new machines installed or new technical
processes used save to reduce costs? Which means,
almost every time, to cut payrolls by firing workers! Finally, there is no sign at all that the little
group in legal control of our 200 greatest corporations will invite that labor participation in general
economic planning which is essential to any reasonable scheme for an economic general staff.

Nevertheless the persistent discussion of planning,
and the fact that big business is strategically and
probably psychologically in a better position than a
multitude of little businesses to play with this idea,
means that we may find ourselves with some sort of
planning commission (or commissions) on our hands
which may at least spy out the land, make public its
findings, and indulge in some useful suggestions. It

could conceivably, as Mr. Chase insists, make forecasts that would advise the investor and so guide investment and credits — a guidance without which planning would be nothing but a joke. It might in like fashion aid the correlation of industries. That would be a beginning, and a beginning on which a society resolved to go socialist might well build. It would at least be a denial of the genius of capitalism with its "automatic laws." It is not likely, however, that any scheme of planning under capitalism would make a forthright attack on the heart of our problem which is the redistribution of the national income. Without this the evils of under-consumption will persist.

The basic truth remains: Before society can plan for general use rather than for private profit it must own or at least control the vital economic enterprises for which it plans. All of which is a way of saying that socialism is the essential condition of planning even as planning is the essential tool of successful socialism. There remains the question whether socialism can impose the requisite degree of planning without the power of an iron dictatorship behind it. This in turn divides into two questions, one political or perhaps psychological, and the other economic. The first is: Can planning coexist with political democracy? The second: Can planning on a scale sufficient to banish unemployment and reduce waste permit any effective degree of consumers' choice, or must we all be rationed, fed, clothed, housed and entertained much as any army is fed, clothed, housed and entertained, with the inevitable corollary that we shall be assigned jobs much as soldiers are assigned jobs.

Neither question can be answered with absolute certainty. Planning under a democracy will succeed in proportion as the democracy is committed to the philosophy of socialism and to the necessity for intelligence in operating it. If these two ideas become dominant, democracy may provide a more orderly and less dangerous way to determine the human desires and prejudices of which even a dictatorship has to take account. Planning in Russia, notably in agriculture, has traced and retraced its steps as a result of Communist Party conflicts and compromises and Stalin's judgment of the strength of peasant resistance. At no time, not even now, could any economic commission, with all the power of the dictatorship behind it, move the masses absolutely as they desired. Nevertheless it will take a democracy capable of understanding and sharing a general interest rather than a democracy immersed in local, sectional and other divisive interests—as our American democracy usually is—to make possible competent and adequate planning. The political democracy that gives sway to log-rolling minorities to make tariff laws and pass pension legislation is not a democracy from which one may hope too much. But then the present democracy is thoroughly capitalist in its philosophy and loyalty.

The other question concerns the possibility of achieving a sufficient degree of economic planning to abolish unemployment without conscripting the workers as producers and rationing them as consumers. I have put this question in an extreme form. Neither the degree of economic planning which served war needs nor the economic planning which serves Russia to-day has entailed conscription and rationing of workers like soldiers. Indeed, the present tendency in Russia seems to be to increase the inducement of differential rewards of labor as opposed to military conscription and to decrease the amount of rationing of goods that has been necessary. If economic planning means even in a transitional period a degree of bureaucratic control which denies consumers' choice and conscripts workers with the aid of the secret police to the degree now practiced in Russia, it will seem well-nigh intolerable to the average American, and it will probably result sooner or later in a dangerous stagnation in the industrial arts. Though I do not think the Russian government gets its astonishing results primarily by terror, I agree, in the main, with Professor Beard's vigorous statement: "One thing, however, is certain: the Russian government rules by tyranny and terror, with secret police, espionage, and arbitrary executions. The system may be adapted to a people who endured

Tsarist despotism for centuries, but to suppose that it could be transported intact to the United States, even if deemed successful in its own bailiwick, is to ignore the stubborn facts of American life and experience—the long practice of self-government in towns, villages, and states, the traditions of personal liberty, the established public school system, and a thousand other elements that stand out like mountains in the American scene."

There is, moreover, a risk that too rigid a degree of planning will break down by its own weight and paralyze initiative by red tape. A machine age, already highly collectivized, must increasingly depend upon the initiative of the engineer rather than of the entrepreneur. But even the initiative of the engineer can be crushed by routine and the rigor of a system which tries the vain task of providing in advance for every conceivable contingency. At present the Russian dictatorship is bringing vigor and imagination to planning. It is easier to apply these qualities to catching up in an industrially backward country than to keeping up. Rather it is easier in some respects to industrialize a country than to manage the production and distribution of the things a nation needs after it is industrialized. Moreover, it is easier for a dictatorship to be vigorous and imaginative and honest in a revolutionary period than when it has settled down. These are not arguments against the success of the Russian experiment; they are reasons why it, and even more certainly any plan in the United States must leave room for meeting emergencies and for developing initiative. Its very perfection on paper may paralyze it.

The best bureaucracy tends to be static and suspicious of those new things and new methods which invention gives us. But I cannot agree with those critics who think economic planning will either completely paralyze the consumers' right to turn from, let us say, coal to oil for domestic heating or will break on a vain attempt at such control. Logically, planning can reckon with change and leave a margin for experimentation. At any rate, there is more reason to expect this adaptability and to work for it than to endure the wastes of a planless economic order for which technological progress is poor compensation.

The hope of a sufficient economic planning to meet the problems of an interdependent society and still permit a high degree of choice of work and consumer goods under a political democracy lies in three things: (1) the possibility of learning the average tendency of consumers' choice and even educating it so that a reasonable forecast can be made of the number of factories necessary for shoes, radios, automobiles, etc.; (2) the fact that the productivity of machinery allows for a very considerable amount of waste from an abstract standpoint without breaking down the system; and (3) that, short of conscription, workers can be guided by information and induced by differential rewards to take the necessary jobs. In a country as far advanced industrially as the United States, a country which does not have to pay to industrialize itself out of its food and clothing, a country already disciplined in factory labor, the degree of rationing and conscription practiced in Russia ought not to be necessary. It would at any rate be impossible without a large scale war.

In short, while production for use rather than profit requires planning, and alone makes possible adequate planning for a machine age, such planning will probably be more aided than hurt by keeping money and the mechanism of profit to permit men a very considerable choice both of what goods they will take and at what jobs they will work. That is to say, workers will be paid in money, and goods will be sold, as they are now by consumers' coöperatives, on a basis of profit, which profit can be refunded either in increased return to the workers, or dividends to purchasers, or reductions of price the next year, or some combination of these methods. At the same time successful planning will enormously enhance the social income of parks, playgrounds, libraries, museums and a hundred and one things that men may enjoy in the increased leisure which the efficient harnessing of the billion wild horses of machinery will give them. But this will require far more than trying to plaster planning on our capitalistic chaos. Important, difficult and deserving of discussion as are questions of the nature of a desirable plan, the way it should be set up and the manner in which its commissions, regional and national, should be constituted, the primary questions for America and the world are not: how shall we plan, but for whom and for what shall we plan? What sort of society do we really want?

LIBERTY'S HARD ROAD

MR. GEORGE BERNARD SHAW has been spending a few pleasant days, including his seventy-fifth birthday, in Russia. His most famous companion was that eminent and charming proletarian, Lady Astor, whose title and whose millions were acquired solely from the proceeds of New York City rents. Mr. Shaw had scarcely sniffed the air of Russia before he began to talk both of Russia and Marxism in terms of eulogy scarcely suggested by his *magnum opus, The Intelligent Woman's Guide to Socialism and Capitalism.* Upon leaving Russia Mr. Shaw assured his hospitable hosts, and the world, that if he were a young man he would settle in Russia, and he advised British youths of eighteen to go to that land of hope.

Now observers who have spent more months or years than Mr. Shaw spent days in Russia have given us good reason for sharing some of his enthusiasms. Very likely thousands of more or less permanently out-of-work young Britishers could, if Russia would admit them, do better there than at home. But somehow the imagination staggers at the thought of a youthful Shaw in the land of Stalin. Could such a congenital rebel get along with the dictatorship?

Would he, more fortunate than some of his socialist comrades, escape prison or exile?

In Mr. Shaw's case, the answer may be yes. He has managed very comfortably to confine rebellion at home to safe and even profitable limits. His opposition to the war was consistent with vigorous disapproval of conscientious objection. He is no theoretical democrat and has lately shown a catholic taste in dictators, ranging from Mussolini to his own stage creation, King Magnus. But Mr. Shaw will not object if instead of joining the army of those who discuss him as author, critic and man, we take him as a type of the individual who does not easily conform, and speculate a bit concerning his fate, not only in Russia but in the world at large during the years that lie ahead.

In other words, how will liberty fare in a world somewhat painfully adjusting itself to the necessary collectivism of a machine age?

We shall make a better approach to our question if we face a few facts fairly and squarely. The first is that the average man to-day would, if he had to choose, gladly exchange most of his theoretical liberties for economic security. This is true not merely because, as we shall see, those liberties are so theoretical, but also because the average man likes to travel with the crowd. He does not want to stray far from his own herd, especially if his herd has good pasture. Moreover there is no tyranny over the mind worse

conscripted for military service or war itself by some domestic dictator like the mad Pilsudski instead of by a foreigner. Often the yoke of the latter in terms of economic burdens and restrictions on personal freedom has been lighter than that of the domestic tyrant, to establish whose rule so many young men have gone to a hideous death. Liberty, interpreted in terms of absolute nationalism, is a denial of common sense and economic reality and menaces our society with destruction. Yet it is in terms of such false liberty that the professional patriot in every country continually talks.

Does it follow, then, that in a world of mob-minded men, where machinery forces specialization and coördination under expert management and governments necessarily increase the area over which thy seek control, liberty is an illusion and the youthful Shaws will do well to accept for at least a generation the best dictatorship they can find? Not unless they want to resign themselves at best to an ant hill society and at worst to a society of ill fed galley slaves.

It would be a needless repetition to labor the case for liberty. It is a social virtue of slow growth. In primitive society all sorts of relations and taboos connected with marriage and the worship of tribal gods forced the most rigid conformity. The struggle for the right "to know, to utter, and to argue freely according to conscience" is not a struggle to recover

what man has lost, but to gain what he never had
save in partial degree. The most we can say is that
certain periods in human history have been less unfavorable to liberty or to certain liberties.

Nevertheless heresy has been the growing point of
society. The right to be one's self and seek one's own
truth and beauty is for earth's choicest spirits the
condition that makes life something more than existence in a prison house. It is the right which lies
at the basis of both art and science. Mr. Shaw's
assertion of that right, especially in his opinion of
what should be men's relations to one another, has
given him significance to our times. The talents of
youthful Shaws can never be best employed over any
long period of time as official eulogists and propagandists of dominant ideas and institutions. Nor will
future history have many less ugly pages than the
past if to be different on those points which the
crowd, or the ruler who controls the crowd, thinks
important, is to subject one's self to punishment surer
and more vindictive than is meted out to the criminal.

But liberty, important as it is, will not be won by
the most eloquent generalizations about it. Rather
it will be useful looking toward the future to draw
up a rough balance sheet of difficulties the realization
of liberty encounters in a world caught in the throes
of revolutionary changes.

The Russia where Mr. Shaw, if he were younger,
would like to live had in some ways an easier time

handling notions of individual freedom because it was unhampered by traditions of liberty. Instead its Tsars had taken it more than once by the throat, as did Peter the Great, to shake it into conformity to some new plan of life. One of the interesting things about its present dictatorship is the care that it takes to educate the whole nation and the skill it has developed in knowing even in Russia when to go and when to stop along some new road. But it is no respecter of persons. The government which exiled the great Trotsky shares with the United States the dishonor of deporting a pathetic little anarchist like Mollie Steiner. Let the immigrant Shaws from Great Britain take notice and watch their step accordingly! The Soviet government has not gone as far as its enemies allege in conscripting workers, but it has not hesitated at one of the most daringly ruthless acts in history: the transplantation of perhaps 1,000,000 peasants, whom it had encouraged to be prosperous, for the crime of relative prosperity. It has sent them thousands of miles from their homes, often without their families. Only a comparatively few of these were guilty of overt acts against the government; by no means all of them were real Kulaks or "tight-fists." They stood or seemed to stand in the way of successful collectivization. The government feared their influence even if they were included in the compulsory collectives. So away they went. Life is abundant in Russia; the birth rate is high; new, more

enlightened, and perhaps happier farmers will take
the places of the exiles in the fields they and their
ancestors long had tilled. By their removal, whenever their removal did not mean open revolt or successful sabotage, the perplexing agricultural problem
was put on its way to solution. But what misery for
the individuals who suffered!

The British Shaws will probably not be peasants.
If they are industrial workers they ought to know
that along with the real concern of the Russian government for making machinery work for the common good, goes a degree of regimentation so great
that Trotsky's friends found that their friendship
for him cost them their jobs and even their fair share
of space in Russia's overcrowded tenements. They
ought to know that the plays and books and poems
they write cannot see the light of day, nor can their
speeches be delivered in any hole and corner out of
reach of the secret police if they offend in any respect which the dictatorship deems important against
the creed which the dictatorship would impose upon
the nation. Have not even the scientists been warned
lest their researches be insufficiently proletarian? As
for old-fashioned rights like habeas corpus, they
simply do not exist.

There is a case for this authoritarian control, a
case powerfully made in its day by the great popes
of the Roman Catholic Church. It is a case that
would give short shrift to the intellectual rebels of

whom Shaw has been commonly taken as an arch type. Granting that nowadays men care more for bread than freedom, granting, too, the hypocritical nature of much of the talk of liberty in the western world, it will take some extraordinary disaster before the men of France, Great Britain or America will docilely accept a dictatorship so logical and so complete as that which now guides the destinies of Russia. To accept it would be counter to the tradition which has given us most of our art and science in the intellectual awakening that followed Europe's dark ages.

But there is far more to the problem of liberty than rejecting undisguised and thoroughgoing dictatorship. A world sick for lack of plan will not run itself. The achievement of any successful reorganization of society means purposeful re-education. Under these conditions men are forced to examine not only our new problems but to re-examine even the older compromises between individual conscience and external authority and between the rival claims of two associations like church and state.

The formula of a free church in a free state was convenient and on the whole has obtained desirable results, especially in America. The form it has taken here is a guaranty of individual freedom of conscience plus the right of men of like mind in religious affairs to form their own associations. But when the Mormons said: "Our religious revelations sanction

polygamy," the state, voicing the customary morals
of the time, said: "Polygamy is immoral and cannot
be sanctioned under guise of religious freedom." The
state won by the convenient circumstance that Mormons, desiring the admission of Utah to the Union,
got at the right moment a new revelation in which
God agreed with the United States. No convenient
new revelation has taught a Baptist professor and an
Episcopalian nurse that they owe the unquestioning
obedience of their conscience as Christians to the
state in any and every war the state may declare.
They, therefore, cannot become American citizens.

If one accepts the Pope's premises, his encyclicals
against birth control and against socialism are logical. They are not in accord either with individual
liberty, or the claims of a socialist state, or of a
non-socialist state which refuses to be bound by the
Catholic conscience in the matter of birth control
legislation. There is no formula in terms of absolutes
to smooth the road. One's sympathies in some of
these and other cases of conflict may be with the
state, in some with the church, and in others with
the individual against both church and state. My
present point is the impossibility in a world of conflicting ideals of any absolute reconciliations. Nevertheless the American *modus vivendi* on freedom of
conscience and of the church has worked tolerably
well and saved us from the burden of an established
church, from such struggles over religion in the

schools as have seriously impaired popular education
in Britain, and from some part at least of the intoler-
ance of ecclesiastical control of government. It is
a line which other and more radical governments,
here and abroad, may well try to follow.

There is a second aspect of the actual achievement
of liberty which also helps to illustrate the difficulty
of solutions by formula. It is in the field of education. Dogmatic rigidity of education is stifling to
individuals and to the discovery of truth. Nevertheless, on its social side education is a process of training the rising generation in the ideas and point of
view which its elders or the dominant group of
them think are wholesome and conducive to social
well-being. The hope of any socialist commonwealth
is in such education. It is nonsense to talk the necessity of purpose and plan in the economic order and
then calmly leave our schools as buttresses of the old
order or turn them over as forums for the haphazard
imparting of ideas teachers happen to hold. Here,
then, is the dilemma. Academic freedom in controversial matters is necessary to good teaching and to
the discovery of truth. Dogmatic, catechetical in-
struction is stifling. In the hands of a dictatorship it
has appalling possibilities for misleading and inflam-
ing the crowd. Contemplation of these possibilities
frighten one in picturing the future of Russia as the
years pass. Yet community standards will always impose limits within which teaching in controversial

matters must be carried on. If anything, a new social order must be more concerned than an old for
the direction and limits of education.

I have never seen any perfect formula for solving
the dilemma. Most attempts achieve verbal rather
than actual solutions. The best one can say is something like this: (1) In our present schools the tendency is to steer clear of controversial issues by
avoiding them rather than by presenting as fairly as
possible different points of view. The result is a
sterilization of education and the production of an
army of morons or social illiterates decorated with
high school and college diplomas. (2) Schools can
educate for a democracy and for a coöperative commonwealth; they can teach the value and purpose
of planning and hold up the great ideals of liberty,
fraternity and equality, without becoming nurseries
of dogmatism and dogmatists. The more confident
we feel in the essential soundness of socialism and
internationalism the more we can hope that they
will prevail wherever and whenever an honest attempt is made to help children and adults to think.

The dilemma between freedom and social authority which we have been discussing in relation to
education runs through our whole society. Likely
enough it will never be perfectly solved until all our
human problems are solved in that dim future when
human striving is ended in the death of our strange
race. But the problems will be less acute as men are

trained in wider coöperation. The law of the machine
is coöperate of perish; but the profits of the machine
go primarily to the few. Hence ours is the coöperation of slaves rather than of free men.

Greater equality may not automatically bring liberty; it may be the equality of robots in a servile
state. But without equality and fraternity as its
companions liberty is doomed. Doubtless the crowd
mind is at its worst when it is the mind of slaves. A
world with larger economic security and equality
will be a world with less envy and malice, far fewer
prizes for successful greed and therefore fewer in-
ducements to the privileged to mislead and exploit
their unprivileged fellows. By so much will the
struggle for equality make possible new meaning and
vision to liberty.

The realist will add one other specific condition of
larger liberty. It is the freeing of the world from
the fear of war. In our world plain fear holds us
in thrall against fair play and freedom. The mon-
strous notion of the absolute sovereignty of the state
which gives it power to conscript men, not for useful
labor, but for killing their fellows, could not last a
day in the minds of men who have suffered incredibly
from it were it not for this fear. It is almost beside
the point to talk real freedom in a world which accepts war, save as a love of freedom may help brave
spirits to defy war itself. In a warlike world the
state in its rôle of protector claims an ultimate vas-

salage from all its citizens which vitiates the whole idea of freedom.

But whatever the realistic conditions for achieving freedom, we must keep alive the idea itself. We may not be able even to give it satisfactory definition in absolute terms. We may have to work for specific *liberties*, like freedom of conscience, of association or the press rather than for *liberty*. Nevertheless, the world will lose something precious, which it has at times envisaged but never wholly gained, if the spirit of freedom which has always inspired the pathfinders should perish from the earth or be crushed in absolute conformity to the bravest attempt at a new social order.

A Catholic biographer of De Soto, one of the most gallant of the men who carried the Spanish flag around the world, speaks of the great release and flaming of energy in Spain following the victories of those loyal Catholics, Ferdinand and Isabella, and the expulsion of Moors and Jews. Such a brilliant period there was, based apparently upon enthusiasm for the Holy Church which held the keys of heaven and marked by its dogmas the road to eternal life. Yet the Spanish Inquisition did not preserve but helped to destroy the glories of that same great Spain. It brought it to pass that the struggle for freedom and ecomonic justice came to be largely identified with revolt against the church. The day following King Alfonso's flight, when Jews could be openly married

been murdered to prevent the truth from coming out; that the police department practiced medieval torture under the name of the third degree and that the vice squad traded in the sale of women's honor; that Tammany's district attorney had been impotent or unwilling to deal with racketeering or remove it from political protection; that the building bureaus were honeycombed with graft; that Tammany was responsible for the "tin box" brigade of public officials with swollen bank accounts that they could not explain in honorable fashion; that the Mayor himself was keeping out of town his confidential financial agent to whom and to a favored applicant for an immensely profitable bus franchise the dapper Mr. Walker entrusted keys to his safe deposit box; that $191,000,000 in "frozen" contracts kept about 100,-000 men out of jobs in a time of desperate need solely because of the incompetence of Tammany officials or their desire to "fix" things before authorized city work could be begun; that a huge and very suspicious bus franchise award was under contemplation with no protection in it for workers against seven days a week work; and that at least ten per cent of a seven hundred million dollar budget was probably a preventable waste.

There is some reason for thinking that this result would not have occurred, at least with so disheartening a majority, if a mayor were to be chosen around whose candidacy a citywide campaign could have been organized. It might not have occurred had the Seabury investigation gathered the cumulative effect it may yet gain.

But even if the city should begin to stir out of the apathy which has made so many moralists mourn and so many cynics rejoice, the spasm of reform in New York, if we may judge the future by the past, is likely to be short-lived. It would be well if we are on the verge of it to examine the situation a little more closely than is the custom of our moralists. Among our moralists I would include the various amusing writers who explain Tammany solely in terms of a corrupt and contented urban democracy and Mr. H. L. Mencken who explains it as the successful recoil to the bluenose Puritan reformer. They have their own ways of telling what New York is. But all of them omit the basic fact that New York is the city where Tammany Hall is the skillful and generally successful broker between the classes with property, power and privilege, and the masses with votes and not much else.

Tammany Hall is the Democratic machine in New York. Technically it rules only in Manhattan, but because of its age and fame the name is often used loosely as I use it here for the closely allied and usually harmonious Democratic machines of the five counties and boroughs in the Greater City. In the Curry-McCooey-Flynn triumvirate (the same being respectively bosses in Manhattan, Brooklyn and the

Bronx), Mr. McCooey gets less fame in the press, especially outside New York, than the size of his borough, the compactness of his power, and the zeal of his devotion to his family entitle him. Nevertheless, with apologies to him and to Eddie Flynn, boss of the Bronx, secretary of state and political liaison officer for Governor Franklin D. Roosevelt, I shall continue for brevity's sake to speak of Tammany in the larger and looser sense of the word.

By the classes in New York I mean not only the fabulous denizens of Wall Street by day and of the narrow lane of Park Avenue by night; not merely the great, the golden and the glamorous whom O. O. McIntyre and Walter Winchell make household words in Oshkosh, but all those more considerable groups, by no means all millionaires, who own most of the land and the public utilities of New York.

By the masses I mean that great polyglot assemblage of white collar and overall workers—when they can get work—who are the New York for whom and of whom *The New Yorker* is not written. Two-thirds of all New Yorkers have family incomes of less than $2500 annually; one-third less than $1500. In a city of millionaires, where apartments are known to rent for $75,000 annually, a million and a half of these masses still live in tenements the like of which it has been illegal for a generation to build.

These definitions and what I am going to say about the things I have defined apply to New York. With changes in detail rather than of principle they apply with equal force to the people, the political machines and the governments of Chicago, Philadelphia and not a few of our smaller cities. In short, I am concerned for a more adequate explanation of the failure not alone of New York, but of our urban democracies in general, than is suggested by cynical, satiric or what-will-you stories about the follies of our people and their delight in the vulgar showmanship of a Bill Thompson or the wise-cracks of a Jimmie Walker.

A recent writer, Mr. Alva Johnston, suggests vividly the secret of Tammany's power when he says: "Father Knickerbocker is like an enormously rich old proprietor who is interested in everything but his estate. He engages Tammany as a steward. He knows that he is going to be robbed, but he would rather be robbed to a reasonable extent than be bothered. At times the steward grows avaricious and begins to impair the estate; Father Knickerbocker flies into a great rage and kicks him out; but after a few years he always takes the old steward back. Father Knickerbocker can be trusted to hang on to Tammany to the very last; it is only when he is on the brink of ruin that he can bring himself to part with his darling but larcenous caretaker."

Now it is captious to press figures of speech too literally. But this, with all its vividness of suggestion, is misleading. It is not a whole city which is the rich

Father Knickerbocker; it is one small part of it. Nor is it the rich part that most loves its larcenous steward. It accepts him as a convenient, even an indispensable agent in the economic and political exploitation of the people. And it accepts him because he has learned the trick of cajoling and intimidating the masses as no aristocratic or obviously plutocratic political organization ever has learned or ever could learn it. He is, or often appears to be a Robin Hood who robs the rich to help the poor, but who nevertheless protects the rich in their privileges.

Popular suffrage in a polyglot urban community early brought it to pass that "the wise, the rich, and the good" could not rule directly. Aaron Burr learned that secret better than Alexander Hamilton more than one hundred and thirty years ago. Tammany Hall had almost a radical origin—at least on the surface. At this moment a red cap, part of its early insignia, adorns the chaste colonial structure which houses the Tammany braves and makes the Hall a not wholly inappropriate witness of the communist demonstrations on Union Square which it faces. Tammany Hall has been guilty of many crimes; it has not been guilty of the fatal blunder of being highbrow or high hat. Its leaders may go in, more than their predecessors, for golf, uptown hotels and Broadway fashions. Do not even the gangsters the same? They may work for their pockets all the time and become wealthy. But they must dodge any taint of snobbery as they would a plague.

Tammany once in its early history was anti-Irish, later it became and still is predominantly Irish-Catholic in leadership and in its most loyal central core. But its skill in managing racial and national prides and jealousies can hardly be exaggerated. The job is not always easy. I remember a year when a political club, predominantly Irish and Jewish, was constrained by political necessity to back an Italian candidate for the Assembly. New York, that year, was in one of its rare reform moods and even in that district the Tammany candidate lost. Choice and vigorous was the language in which the old-timers expressed their opinion of "the wop" for losing. Nevertheless, the Italian migration into that district continued. Tammany renominated "the wop"—who was an able politician—the next year and he began a political career which carried him far. In other words, Tammany knows better than to let prejudice stand in the way of profit.

Along with Tammany's calculated shrewdness in giving to every national group enough representation to keep it happy goes a genuine sense for the current of life on the sidewalks of New York. Tammany is not so much kind or generous as it is human in its contacts. At its very rare and occasional best this human understanding finds expression in the honest social interest of a man like Senator Robert Wagner who would, I think, have very little difficulty in belonging to a labor or possibly a moderate Socialist party if it were strong enough to offer him a political future.

Even on its lower planes this human feeling permits Tammany legislators rather more easily than certain so-called "respectables" to support welfare legislation so long as it does not threaten the political racket which they conduct. Aside from general social legislation, Tammany district leaders and the precinct captains below them have to be friendly and approachable and ready to do small favors at inconvenient times. In a city as impersonal and bewildering as ours, the friendship of some politicians in the hierarchy which extends from precinct captains up to the big boss himself is like the shadow of a great rock in a weary land. No organization is ever likely permanently to defeat Tammany which does not in its own way come in equally close contact with the people.

At the same time the rôle of Tammany or any other city machine as the friend of the poor is grossly exaggerated. Tammany has never minded how much the poor have paid directly or indirectly in rotten housing, in organized vice and in excessive charges for gas and electricity to groups with which Tammany has very profitable relationships. Its district leaders not only occupy well paid city jobs at which

they do not work but by common report grow rich
on direct or indirect exploitation of the drug trade,
speakeasies, commercialized vice, the purchase of land
by the city, the awarding of city contracts, the nomination of judges and the administration or maladmin-
istration of justice. From these things the poor are
the chief sufferers.

The amazing part of it is that the poor know this
and dislike it. Over and over I have heard it admitted
by the very folk who vote for Tammany. It is a
respectable middle-class delusion that the masses are
completely fooled. The reason for their vote is partly
the almost universal cynicism and despair among the
masses; more largely and concretely it is the bitter
fact that Tammany forges out of the very miseries of
the people the chains to bind them. Never was that
more true than now. In a country like ours, without
automatic relief for the unemployed through general
unemployment insurance or indemnification, municipal relief or temporary jobs, distributed from political club houses, are used as a flagrant and open bribe.
Often not actual relief, miserable as that is, but the
hope of it, is the bribe. These facts have been brought
into the open in the Seabury inquiry. There is no
greater fallacy than that economic depression always
automatically and rapidly makes rebels. Its first effect
is often to make slaves; to reduce men to the level of
dogs kept grateful to their masters by a few bones
from the very game they have killed for them.

Tammany knows how to crack the whip as well as toss a bone. In many districts Tammany rules at least as much by sheer force as by friendship. That fear extends from the property owner afraid of assessments to the pushcart peddler and the tenement dweller; from the big merchant to the army of job holders who do not feel secure even if theirs are civil service positions. And these people, hopeful of the bone or fearful of the whip, do not forget to register and vote!

Over and over again on Election Day I have had complaints of this or that type of vote-stealing—in which, by the way, Tammany usually has the connivance of the feeble Republican machine—and nearly always the complainant is afraid to make an affidavit. He has a brother, a son or a cousin who might suffer somehow. He is a small storekeeper whom the police could drive out of business under the guise of enforcing municipal ordinances. He is, perhaps, a pushcart peddler wholly dependent upon the mercy of the powers that be. I remember one election when a Tammany captain deliberately looked behind the curtain of a voting machine—a very common practice —and when he found that the voter had pulled down one Socialist lever, although all the rest were Democratic, this captain followed the poor man out into the street to tell him that no longer could he sell from his cart anywhere in that district.

Actual gang violence probably plays less part in

intimidation in New York than in former years in Chicago, but there is plenty of it. There are districts where I have seen an unholy alliance of gangsters and politicians, with a magistrate or judge or two in the offing, operating in and outside of the school buildings in which the votes were cast. Everybody knew who they were and what they were doing there. Long ago the magistrates of New York have made a joke of the election law. Not many years ago one of New York's magistrates refused even to hold for the grand jury a Tammany worker, herself an election inspector, who was caught voting the third time. Under these circumstances the average voter in working class districts is likely to think twice before offending the ubiquitous organization with such immense powers of reward and punishment in its own hands and in the hands of its underworld allies.

The popular attitude was expressed by a citizen who accosted me as I was waiting for belated police help to end outrageous intimidation in a certain polling place in the election of 1931. I was on the street, a little distance from the school house—fit scene for education in practical politics! For the moment things were quiet. The citizen said: "Mr. Thomas, you're wasting your time. None of us dares vote here as he thinks. Dutch Shultz [a famous racketeer and beer runner] has his men all through this district." Whether or not this was completely true— and later I heard the charge from others—it shows the fear which Tammany and its well-rewarded underworld allies inspire.

In thus dispensing rewards and punishment, Tammany's control of the lower courts is of peculiar importance. With very few exceptions magistrates and municipal court judges are among the most valuable cogs in the Democratic political machine. Far more serious even than the price they pay for jobs or than the low caliber of some of them, is their well-nigh absolute dependence upon the district leader who is usually responsible for their appointment or election. All judges, especially in the lower courts, have an immense area in which to apply discretion. Their decisions are not so obviously wrong that they can easily be upset. They can always claim that their mistake was at least an honest error in judgment.

It is in this field that the so-called contract system operates. The magistrate or judge secretly gets a request from a district leader or a well-known fixer or a court clerk in touch with the district leader, to let this man go, to hold this man but not that for the grand jury, etc. Magistrate Harry Gordon once publicly charged that many of his colleagues took lists into court with them on which the disposition of cases was marked in advance. There is a famous story in New York of a certain Special Sessions judge, now no longer in office, who never trusted his memory but used to mark his calendar in pencil. One morning, in his temporary absence from the bench, a colleague rubbed out the original marks and put some very different ones on the calendar. It was two or three weeks before the resulting confusion was cleared up and some Tammany henchmen were let out of jail. A policeman once told me in all seriousness that if policemen did not "treat gangsters rough" and maybe give them a little taste of the third degree, gangsters would go around "spitting on the cops," for, said he, almost all of them have their fixers and are never held by the magistrates.

Some district leaders are more active than others in manipulating the law. One well-known leader is not only said to have peculiar influence over magistrates, but peculiar power to open prison doors all the way up to Sing Sing, where he is said frequently to be the honored guest of prison officials. This same district leader is supposed to be the particular patron of the infamous drug traffic on Welfare Island—a traffic which is said to be growing enormously despite the honest efforts of Commissioner Patterson to stamp it out.

Now the sinister relation between the courts and the political machine is known, and admitted by every lawyer who practices in the lower courts. Yet, until very lately, the Bar Association has ignored the whole matter. Even now the Seabury investigation only in the Silbermann case has established legal proof of the contract system which every well-informed reporter and lawyer knows exists. No one can explain the power of Tammany who ignores the degree to which the legal profession in New York has been prostituted from the service of justice to the pursuit of fees. Gangs and rackets in New York could not last a year if it were not for political and legal protection of an overt and positive sort which lawyers, some of them on their way to be judges and leading men in their profession, willingly bestow, for a price, upon these men who are known to be public enemies.

Yet, save at very rare intervals, the leaders of the profession ignore or condone these practices. They have their own special interests to protect. They may object to ambulance chasers, but they do no crusading against the political system which leaves them free to serve those great interests and powerful individuals whom wealth has long since rendered immune from the ordinary criminal or even civil law in America.

It was something more than an ironic accident, it was a parable of the times, that the able Isidor Kresel, scourge of ambulance chasers and a terror to guilty magistrates, should himself be under six or seven indictments in connection with the failure of the Bank of United States. In saying this I am not prejudging the question of Mr. Kresel's legal guilt or innocence. It is possible that he has a moral defense that has not yet been heard. It is certain that the vigor of the Steuer and Tammany attack on him arose at least in part from personal and political considerations which demanded that Mr. Kresel be discredited.

Nevertheless, as the average poor man in a year of hard times sees the situation, here is a man who was the enemy of wrongdoing in magistrates' courts and yet was himself the brains of the system by which a bank with a misleading name and an elaborate structure of affiliates juggled the money of its depositors for the profit of its directors. There was on the whole more popular wrath in New York at the collapse of the Bank of United States than over the wrongdoing in magistrates' courts. So far, in the popular mind, Mr. Kresel's indictment increases and justifies the general cynicism of voters who say, "Well, in New York everybody's after what he can get. The respectables are as bad as Tammany. I'll stick with Tammany. Anyway I know the district leader." As a young man said to me in all seriousness, following a meeting at which I had discussed the lack of any difference between the old parties, "I think there is a difference. Tammany passes around the graft better."

Come to think of it, why should the average man who has an income of less than $2500 a year get excited about the conventional notion of clean government? To him it seems a remote thing, perhaps a hypocritical thing. Municipal housecleaning is usually directed against illegitimate graft and rackets, not against the deep-rooted and legitimate "racket" of private landlordism which is responsible for the slum, the ugliness and the discomfort of the city. I do not criticize landlords as individuals when I say that landlordism by appropriating rents on land values created by society not only bars the way to the city beautiful, but is indirectly responsible for the vice and crime and misery which bad housing, unnecessary congestion and lack of parks and playgrounds create.

Until the present depression, the rise in land values alone in New York City equaled or exceeded the huge budget of the city year after year. Why should we expect the people of the city to become excited over waste and graft in the budget so long as they have to support this enormous load of landlordism, the beneficiaries of which are often the very "respectables" who urge reform? And why should the "respectables" who urge reform be too bold in urging it when Tammany can so easily strike back at them by increasing the assessments on the property they own or denying them the rewards on property which the city may condemn? Was it not by this sort of threat that Boss Tweed compelled the ruling Astor of his day to sign a pitiful statement whitewashing the Tweed ring?

These queries become more pertinent when one remembers that the usual agent of those conventionally interested in good government in New York is the Republican Party. The voters of New York may not be masters of political science, but they know the rec-

ord of the Republican Party in Washington and
Albany; they have heard of the oil scandals and of the
way tariffs are made. What is more, they know all
about the local Republican machine. They know it
plays jackal for the Tammany tiger most of the time;
that is, it is satisfied with the crumbs that Tammany
has to drop under a bipartisan system. These crumbs
plus some federal patronage have long nourished the
Koenig machine to a kind of anæmic life. New York
has too much sense of humor seriously to think of this
machine as a remedy for, or an alternative to, Tammany Hall.

The subservience of the Republican machine—
though not, of course, of all Republicans—was never
so glaringly illustrated as in 1931. Instead of trying
to capitalize the Seabury discoveries, the Republican
machine in three boroughs, Brooklyn, Queens and
Richmond, went in with the Democrats on a deal
whereby it got five out of twelve new judgeships—at
least seven of them unnecessary. In Manhattan the
Republican leader, Mr. Samuel Koenig, whose brother
adorns the bench by grace of Tammany, obliged his
Tammany friends by nominating that perfect "set
up," Colonel E. C. Carrington, who while the campaign was on, was shown by Judge Seabury to have
hired Judge George Olvany, then the Tammany boss,
and barely to have stopped short by advice of counsel
from bribing the dock commissioner in an effort to
get almost five times the assessed value of a decrepit

pier from the city. Colonel Carrington's general record could not have been unknown to the shrewd Mr. Koenig even if the details of it were uncovered after his nomination.

Still worse is the fact that in New York as in many other great American cities the official labor movement which ought to be the backbone of the struggle against corruption, extortion and privilege, is tied up with the political racketeers. Year after year the Central Trade and Labor Council in New York goes through the solemn farce of endorsing on non-partisan grounds the Tammany ticket—this in the face of Tammany's bad record in the matter of the padrone system in the cleaning of public schools, the seven-day week in the subways, its failure to enforce the prevailing rate of wages law on city contracts, etc. This endorsement is rewarded by political favors for the leaders and friendly connivance in their own rackets, as well as by occasional political help against the legal and illegal devices of employers to beat strikes. This kind of help in time of strike amounts to little, far less than justice, but in a country where law is in the hands of the strong this little favor sometimes brings even the more progressive unions more or less tacitly to heel behind Tammany.

Just how many rank and file votes go with the endorsement of the labor leaders is hard to say, for some of these leaders are endured by the rank and file as a necessary or at any rate an inescapable evil. But this in turn foments new cynicism about trusting anyone in authority to serve the general good. "What is the use," the workers say, "when even some of our own leaders, yes, even in the more progressive unions, use strong arm men and job control and all the tricks of Tammany to keep their power? Can we trust anybody no matter what he promises?"

This is not the place to discuss in detail the degradation of labor unionism by racketeering, nor to explain how it has sprung out of our political and economic situation. One illustration of the political tie-up may be in order.

There is in New York and ought to be an organization of moving picture operators. In numbers some 1,300 members with 500 wholly irregular or permit men who pay dues for the privilege of working at a low scale without any voice or vote in the union. The president of this organization received in 1930 $47,500 in salary and a "gift," not counting union perquisites besides all he makes as head of a non-union manufacturing company. He maintains his power largely by job control and, it is alleged, by a strong arm squad. He put eight expensive sound and picture trucks at union expense but, it is said, without union authorization, in the service of the Democratic campaign of 1930. Sheriff "Tin-box" Tom Farley and other politicians are commonly believed to be his friends. No wonder he has heretofore enjoyed almost complete legal immunity! The saddest part of the story is that the so-called official opposition to him is tarred with the same sort of stick.*

While this is not by any means typical of all A. F. of L. unions it is not without parallels. The greatest tragedy of New York and other big city politics is that *official* labor so largely seems even to its own rank and file on the side of privilege and allied with the powers that prey. No superficial reform will touch this evil. Labor unions we must have and have them on the right side in any economic or political struggle to build in time the new society which must rise from our crumbling order. That requires a revolution in ideals against the poison of racketeering with which our American acquisitive society is sick.

From a combination of these two facts—the unwillingness of the "respectable" element including, alas, many labor leaders, to put up a real fight against Tammany, and the refusal of exploited workers to see anything particularly significant for them in a fight simply against Tammany's illegal graft—arises the futility of the so-called reform movement in New York. In the twenty-five years I have lived in or near the city I have never seen a genuinely well-organized, enthusiastic, root and branch, "good government" fight against Tammany. I have never seen a reasonably intelligent effort on the part of the reform ele-

---

*Since this paragraph was written, under various sorts of pressure some progress has been made in this particular union. No $25,000 gift went to the president, the election was fairly conducted and promises were given of proper recognition of permit men. The organization still represents "business" unionism of which, alas, there are worse examples in New York and other cities.

ment to dramatize its own case and its own occasional achievements.

I do not except the Mitchel administration. Mr. Mitchel and his colleagues were elected because there was a split in the Democratic machine and bitter resentment against the reigning boss, Charlie Murphy, for the impeachment of Governor Sulzer. The reformers did not present to the city a well-thought-out program of health, education, taxation, control of public utilities and so on. The campaigning that aroused the city was negative, and the most significant participant in it was John Hennessey with his little black book from which he read charge after charge against Tammany.

In office the Mitchel administration did some good things. It did not tackle the problem of landlordism or the position of public utilities. It failed to impress the public with its own achievements and it went out in a confusion of religious, racial and war issues. Since that time until the present year there has never been anything but futility on the part of reformers. Outstanding men avoided a mayoralty nomination from the reform element as they would avoid smallpox. In 1925, Mr. Waterman, the pen manufacturer, was something like the fourteenth man approached. His campaign lacked everything: knowledge, ideas, conviction, enthusiasm, showmanship.

Major La Guardia in 1929 was a far abler and more colorful candidate. It was an open secret that he got little support from the usual reform crowd and that what support was given him simply tended to water down and weaken the strength of the constructive ideas he may have had. It is impossible to believe that men of the strength and ability who are nominally to be found in anti-Tammany ranks could make such a mess of their own reform campaign if they were vigorously and genuinely in earnest.

The forces which consciously or subconsciously operate to hold back these well-to-do or wealthy respectables were put in a nutshell by former Ambassador Gerard. He, if he was correctly quoted in the press, once told the assembled bond salesmen who seek sanctuary from one another in the Harvard Club that they ought to be grateful to Tammany for protecting them from municipal socialism. Something of the same idea in other circumstances and in another form was voiced by the urbane and dapper Jimmie Walker himself. In 1924, the year before Al Smith made him Mayor, presumably to the Governor's lasting regret, Mr. Walker (then a State Senator), a Republican Congressman from California, and I were speaking at a rather select club symposium in Brooklyn on the issues of the Presidental campaign. The California Congressman worked the Red menace overtime. Mr. Walker, in his own inimitable fashion, ridiculed his argument and ended by turning to his Republican adversary and saying, "Why, Congress-

man, we know the people and we know just how
much to give them." There is the secret of it.

The moral of my tale I hope is plain. Tammany
may now and again be temporarily defeated because
it gets careless. It might come to more serious grief
were it, like the Republican Party in Chicago, to be
divided into warring factions. It will not be permanently defeated, nor will a much better government be set up in New York, until there is awakened
in the heart of the people a new conception of the
immense importance of city government, and a new
concept of what city government may mean to general well-being. But the city government which has
meaning and worth for the lives of our people must
have behind it a philosophy and program to challenge
the prevailing cynicism. It must handle the problem
of landlordism, public utilities and education with
new power and new vigor. It cannot leave unchal-
lenged the rights of those who now exploit the workers under capitalism and use Tammany to keep them
quiet politically. The only successful and worthwhile
challenge to Tammany Hall is the municipal socialism which has been so potent a factor in European
cities and has done so much to make Milwaukee, in
spite of its propinquity to Chicago, the best governed
city in America.

In affirming this conviction I do not disguise the
value of an awakening of the popular conscience

against corruption. I admit the importance of considering the machinery and structure of city government.

With a characteristic American faith in an external or formal panacea, some editors and leaders of public opinion in America insist that the City Manager plan which has worked tolerably well in smaller cities and amazingly well in Cincinnati, not long ago among the worst of our cities, is the one sufficient hope for cities like New York and Philadelphia. Obviously this cannot be true if our diagnosis of what is wrong in New York is anywhere near right. It is not true in the light of the somewhat checkered history of the plan in Cleveland and elsewhere. City government is more than a matter of "efficient" administration or conventional "good" government. Efficient for what, good for whom? For real estate interests and public utilities? For its own ends and the ends of the privileged groups generally, Tammany is amazingly efficient—so efficient that it could easily capture the council which under the City Manager plan shapes policy and chooses the manager. Indeed, I think, given the huge size of New York and the psychology of its voters that it would be harder to arouse the public by a campaign for a council than for a mayor. "Off years" when no mayor is elected are always especially easy for Tammany. The structure of New York's government should be improved. This requires abolishing five expensive counties in one city and consolidating some borough offices. It could be done without a city manager and would not necessarily be done with one. Indeed, New York does not primarily suffer from bad governmental machinery or lack of brains in her officials, but from wrong policies.

The outstanding virtue of the City Manager plan is less in itself than in the idea of proportional representation in the council which usually, though not always, accompanies it. Emphatically proportional representation would make for democracy and efficiency even if Tammany captured the majority of seats. It could be had to some degree in our New York government without a city manager.

This is not summarily to reject consideration of a City Manager plan. It is, however, to reject one feature commonly associated with it. Most advocates of the City Manager plan add that it also should be accompanied by "non-partisanship." That notion is dangerously fallacious unless one simply means that ordinary Republican or Democratic political divisions are worthless in the city (so are they for the matter of that in the nation!). But we cannot get along without party in the true sense of the word. Tammany can never be kept down except by an enduring organization which ought, to be sure, to appeal to other and less crass motives than Tammany, but which must be based on friendly contacts with the people. I have heard Cincinnati's encouraging progress in municipal righteousness cited as proof of the non-partisanship city government. Actually one reason for the much greater success of the City Manager plan in Cincinnati than elsewhere—Cleveland, for instance—is the fact that the group that originally won the new charter stuck together and has acted as *a party* in municipal campaigns and between times. No mere city party will be enough permanently to do the job in our greatest cities.

In the long run no city party, least of all in New York, can be divorced from the prevailing philosophy, program and organization of American federal and state politics. Neither the ideals nor the program which will save New York can exist and make headway irrespective of the ideals and program that prevail in the nation. The worst that can be said of Tammany is that it has taken over the anything-to-win, grab-bag ethics of capitalist economics. The philosophy we want cannot stop at the city line. It is impossible to outline a plan for municipal housing, for dealing with public utilities or improving education which does not require action at Albany as well as at City Hall. In short, the price of municipal good government in a huge city like New York is a sincere and conscious devotion to principles and to a program of emancipation from poverty and exploitation which go far beyond mere opposition to Tammany Hall.

In my judgment what we Socialists were able to do in 1929, in spite of lack of organization and the means to finance an intensive campaign, shows that people

can be interested in a city government which touches
their lives and the lives of their children so intimately
and constantly that what it does and leaves undone
matters more than any man's individual effort. It is
this sort of work that must be kept up; and if a declaration of personal faith is in order I want to make it
clear that I am comparatively little interested simply
in cleaning up New York, and that I have little faith
in what will be accomplished by an emotional spasm
of reform. My deep interest in New York City and
elsewhere is in a new order of social life, a new sense
of the necessity of coöperation, a new art of living
together. To attain that victory means an attack
upon an economic and political order of which Tammany Hall is only one of the symptoms.

THE CHURCHES AND THE END OF AN EPOCH

"IT IS the greatest irony in history that the most militaristic and acquisitive nations in the world should have chosen a pacifist Jewish peasant not only as their prophet but as their God." So a thoughtful Jewish judge told me thirteen years ago when we were discussing the fate of conscientious objectors in the World War.

From this central paradox or irony of Christianity spring lesser paradoxes. Thus, ever since Constantine brought Christianity into unholy wedlock with the state, Christianity in its dominant or official forms has usually been a bulwark of the status quo, deserving on the whole of the celebrated Marxian denunciation of religion as "the opium of the peoples." Yet a primitive type of Christian communism has persisted from apostolic times down to the last of the Shaker communities or to the long-established community of Amana, Iowa. In the main stream of church tradition, both Catholic and Protestant, there has been a long line of those deeply concerned for the Kingdom of God on earth. Saints, in or out of the church, like Francis of Assisi, Tolstoi and Gandhi, have acknowledged their debt to Jesus of Nazareth. Historically European socialism has been at least non-religious and usually bitter against the church, yet the socialism of many British labor leaders has had some of its roots in non-conformist chapels, and in America such sound and uncompromising radicalism as that of Walter Rauschenbusch and Harry F. Ward has been definitely Christian in origin. The Christian Bible itself, on which innumerable tyrants have taken their coronation vows or oaths of office, contains more bitter and extreme criticism of despoilers of the people, of the wealthy and the respectable than any radical tract. "Go to, ye rich, weep and howl for the woes that come upon you" was not written by Karl Marx. I have often wondered whether some homespun Southern preacher from the hills may not yet make devastating use in a mill town strike of the Epistle of James, the Book of the Prophet Amos or even of the Sermon on the Mount according to St. Luke.

It is against this background of obvious fact about a religion which in the main has been an opiate yet carries even in its sacred books so much dynamite, that we must examine the problem of Christianity and the churches in relation to the social order.

The problem will not be solved by the current humanistic version of Protestant Christianity—which to tell the truth has not been particularly useful in any social struggle of which I have knowledge. I doubt whether humanism is a valid religion. It is scarcely a valid development from Christianity. The main concern of Christianity has been, is now and must be with the question of God: does He exist, what is His nature and what His relation to men. If modern Christianity has any unique and significant contribution to the social order it is to establish the truth of its conception of God as love. That is a problem both of philosophy and of life. Atheism or agnosticism springs at least as much from observation of human conduct, including the conduct of Christians, as from contemplation of the universe that astronomy, physics, chemistry and biology give us. Christianity has no economics or political service for our guidance; it has certain great ethical principles perhaps more explicitly and clearly stated and exemplified in the Jesus of the Gospels than in other religions. But if we can tell anything at all about the mind of Jesus it is clear that for him these ethical principles were derived simply and directly from his sense of God. Whatever one may think of the learned discussions of the "apocalyptic hope" and the "interim ethic" in the teachings of Jesus, it seems to me clear that his way of life, his exhortations to forgiveness, to mercy, to brotherhood, in short to an unworldly perfection, were based on his belief in One who forgives us as we forgive others, whose mercy is everlasting, whose Fatherhood is the ground of human brotherhood and who is Himself perfection.

There are dozens of more powerful reasons for a decent code of social ethics or for a new economic order than Christianity in the more extreme of its modern versions can give us. If Jesus was mistaken about God we may admire him as we admire many another of the prophets and saints of all religions and of none; we cannot reasonably accept his ethics as authoritative.

On the other hand, if a man does accept in any sincerity a faith in Jesus and Jesus' God, whether he calls himself orthodox or modernist, it is impossible to see how he can be at peace with the present social order whose God is profit and whose largest social loyalty is the inadequate and divisive loyalty of nationalism. That Christianity has survived so many centuries of giving its support to the exploitation of men, first by feudalism and then by capitalism, that it has not long since perished in the shame of its blessing upon wars which set Christian to killing Christian brother—this is no proof of the divinity of its origin, but of the strength of the pitiful superstition and hungry credulity of a bewildered humanity. The complacent boast I have heard from preachers that Islam was the religion of the sword but Christianity of the cross, may be true of the mind of their founders but it is untrue to historic fact concerning the religions. Christianity has had its devoted missionaries —so has Islam—but its extension in Europe was due to the swords of Charlemagne and lesser warriors. By the sword and the gun were the unfortunate Indians converted by the Spaniard—when they were not killed; by the most despicable slave trade in history were African Negroes brought to the American Christ. Islam in Spain was tolerance itself compared to the Catholicism that drove it out. In the last century Protestant and Catholic missionaries too often have been advance agents of western imperialism. Islam has accepted men of all races who embrace it as equals—a thing which even modern missionary Christianity has not achieved in practice. The cruelest wars in history were fought between Christian sects and when men's real religion became nationalism, priests and ministers obligingly invoked the wrath of God on other nationals as once they had done on infidels and heretics. To-day Christianity which always blesses war furnishes its chaplains to prisons where men are simply confirmed in crime, and builds its cathedrals with the profits of successful gambling in Wall Street. Yet if words mean anything, all this is sheer apostasy to its God and the absolute negation of its gospel of brotherhood. This apostasy is becoming slowly clearer to great masses of workers in all countries as it has long been clear to a small minority of Christians. The patient masses are not likely to be forever put off with the sorrowful confession: Christianity after nineteen centuries has not yet been tried. Unless it is tried, and that immediately and on a large scale, the cry will become ever louder: Away with this organized hypocrisy which so long has made us endure our unnecessary miseries and has blessed the means of our destruction by lulling us with threats and promises of an unknown hereafter.

At this point some readers will want to tell me that in spite of its failures, even of its apostasy, Christianity has immensely improved and softened social relations and that we owe to it whatever is good in western civilization. I have not space to argue the matter at length nor is it altogether relevant to my main contentions. Unquestionably official Christianity, as I said in my opening paragraphs, has not wholly escaped the influence of its own gospels and it has carried with it the standard by which its enemies have judged it. Certainly it had an educational and civilizing effect upon barbarous Europe. Yet there has been great exaggeration about the reforms Christianity ostensibly has brought and the degree of its responsibility for them. For example, economic forces had more to do than Christianity with the rise of our imperfect democracy. It is not scientific and it is irritating to hear clergymen smugly credit to Christianity intellectual progress and social reform which their churches consistently fought. Even so devout a Christian as Lord Shaftesbury continually mourned that in his fight for tolerable factory conditions the saints were against him, the sinners with him.

This indictment to the sincere believer in a mighty God and a true gospel cannot be other than a challenge. It is dubious business for the convinced believer to leave the church altogether simply because he is heartsick over its failure as a constructive revolutionary force. Rather he will work to swell the ranks of what the Hebrew prophets called in Israel "the righteous remnant."

What will such a man say? That to be a Christian one must be a socialist? Not necessarily. To be a good socialist in our present society is, indeed, easier than to be a good Christian. Socialism does not, like Christianity, say "give to him that asketh of thee." Socialism, as Bernard Shaw and others have pointed out, calls men to work out a new social order, not to personal renunciation save as that may be involved in the social struggle. Tolstoi's life was an attempt to carry out immediately the full ethic of the gospels, not of socialism. If it was, as I think, a glorious failure; if a general imitation of Tolstoi's bread labor would bring our modern machine age society to disruption and starvation, the fault was not in Tolstoi, but in the impossibility of living out so completely Christian an ethic in an interdependent society based on economic principles which are the denial of a Christian ethic. Men will continue to fail as Christians in an unChristian order. The Christian keen enough to discern the compromises forced on him despite his best intentions has peculiar reason for wanting the coöperative commonwealth. He should, indeed, set himself some standards of conduct and recognize some compromises which he cannot make and keep house with himself. But in an economic order where production is for profit and exploitation is inherent in it, he cannot wholly escape by any renunciation short of suicide. And suicide is defeat. The man who says that he lives by the Golden Rule only conceives life in its visible personal relations. He has no conception of how completely the Golden Rule is denied by the rule of gold which is the master of economic life.

Nevertheless, while I think socialism is the best road to a Christian social order, another man with at least equal force—so far as the gospels are concerned—may urge Tolstoi's type of individualistic anarchy, or something like Kropotkin's communistic anarchy. The ethics of Christianity at its best and the kind of God it professes to accept as Lord of Life, are, as I have argued, wholly incompatible with capitalism and its god profit. But Christianity does not of itself give us a program for managing the machine age. It does not even give us detailed wisdom for guiding our own lives in that machine age. Socialism has a definite relation to modern methods of distribution and production and a fairly definite program for a new society. It is a loose use of words to say that Jesus or Plato or any of the Hebrew prophets was the first socialist. And the question "What would Jesus do?" even for the sincere Christian, does not permit precise answer in circumstances so immensely different from his own. That is to say, while our present social order is a denial of Christianity, only here and there made more tolerable by it, and while Christianity for the believer should be a mighty force for justice, it is not, even for the believer, of itself a sufficient basis for constructive change.

The "back to Jesus movement" has inevitably lost much of its power. Partly this is true because modern criticism which began by seeking to make Jesus more real has left us little assurance about what he himself did and taught. Partly it is true because it tried the impossible task of urging us to accept Jesus' ethics while questioning his theology. Most of all it is true because the experience and teaching of one man living in a particular time and place and undertaking one task cannot be made the main foundation for the social structure of a different time. Whatever inspiration we may get out of the great story of the Galilean peasant, who left his work and who avoided family responsibility to preach the Kingdom of God, it is an unscientific waste of time to try to find in, or read into, his life economic and political principles which must take account of scores of factors with which he was necessarily unfamiliar. As one looks objectively at our modern social problems one cannot see that Christians get a much better guidance for solving them by going back to Jesus than Jews from their prophets, or than Buddhists might get from Buddha.

If this is true of professing Christians how much more true is it of the hosts of men who with indiffer-

ence or with sorrow must reject a Christian theology,
even of a liberal sort, and yet want to get rid of poverty and tyranny and war. Even if Christian socialism
were not a term in Europe for a party neither Christian nor socialist I should not urge the formation or
growth of a self-styled Christian socialist group in
America. That is not the basis for unity. If a man's
Christianity makes him a socialist, well and good.
But let him remember it does not absolve him from
an understanding of economic forces and programs
in which non-Christians may unite with him. Let
him prove the values his Christianity gives by his
service in the socialist movement not by trying to substitute Mark for Marx. (If dogmatic Marxism has
some of the unfortunate qualities of dogmatic Christianity it will be corrected by a more scientific approach to facts, not by another dogmatic theology.)

But if Christianity cannot be made an adequate
basis of, or substitute for, a modern social philosophy
and program, it does not follow that sincere Christians are justified in confining themselves to large and
rather sentimental generalizations about brotherhood.
Those generalizations are meaningless unless worked
out in a world where there is one justice for the rich
and another for the poor, where gross inequalities of
wealth and poverty have little relation to need or deed
and none at all to brotherhood. Christians as Christians must discuss not only particular crimes of society like the Mooney-Billings case but the general

nature of our social order. A fearless preacher may
have to guard against dogmatism or confess that he is
not an expert in this field or that; he certainly must
guard against an ecclesiastical attempt to dictate to
society from the vantage point of the church. But he
must discuss in the light of his faith the social order
which holds us all enchained if he has a faith worth
bothering about. And the same sort of duty rests on
the layman.

Outstanding men in pew and pulpit are doing this
very thing. That is good, but the promise of their
power does not seem great. I doubt if they can win
their own organizations. I have some hope of what
the churches might do but very little for what they
will do. I believe the church will bless the next war,
which it is doing little to prevent, as it has blessed all
wars—this despite the fact that the now famous
World Tomorrow questionnaire encourages hope that
an impressive number of clergymen will be conscientious objectors.

I have recently seen the Protestant church once
again miss a magnificent opportunity in the industrial
struggle. The strikers at Danville, Virginia, were
Protestant church folk and truly religious. They
opened their meetings with prayer. The president of
the company was also a Protestant churchman. Almost without exception the churches of Danville and
of the South stood by the president who fought
against any union organization of the workers. A

very gallant struggle was lost, and with the defeat the hope of peaceful social progress in the industrialization of the South grows dimmer. Fine voices in the church were raised in the crisis, but the church was impotent or indifferent on an issue involving not primarily economics but human justice and liberty.

We are nearing the end of an epoch. To that all signs point. Must the epoch die in bloody chaos? Can a new epoch be born only out of the bitter mass discipline of dogmatic communism? Conceivably the churches still are powerful enough to help us find a less violent answer. They might do it not by preaching a hard economic and political creed, but by inspiring clergy and laity to seek a human meaning for their version of the Kingdom of Heaven on earth. Under this insipration we might ideally come near to achieving "a revolution by consent," or at least to waging our economic struggle in some atmosphere of fair play which would lessen bitterness and strife.

For so great a service I see little sign of hope in churches. At any rate, whether for good or evil, their influence is steadily waning. The decline of the Russian church is breath-taking in its rapidity and would have been impossible save for its natural weakness. Our Western Roman Catholic church is amazingly on the defensive in the Spain of the republic, in Latin America, and to no small extent in Fascist Italy. It will take more than encyclicals to check the practice of birth control or the growth of socialism. At that, the historic church's magnificent organization, its knowledge of the human soul, its ancient and impressive ritual, guarantee it a better hope of earthly immortality than a divided and sorely perplexed Protestantism. But Catholic or Protestant, if the churches cannot rise to their present social opportunity in the light of their best traditions—rather than their worst —better let them die. Religion of some sort—as the strength of the secular religion of communism proves —will not die with the churches. Nor will the memory of the saints. And in the meanwhile there is that fine minority in the churches of those whose religion makes them crusaders for plenty and peace, freedom and fellowship. Their work cannot be wholly vain. Of that minority there cannot be too many and to that minority though I cannot share its faith and give it my allegiance I offer my admiration and respect.

FAITH OF MY FATHERS

IT IS no longer the fashion among our intellectuals to use "Puritan" as a general and inclusive term of scorn and abuse. Recent historians have instead given us a much fairer picture of a people with great faults but greater virtues, possessed not only of an integrity but a culture not to be despised.

But for what is sometimes called the decadent Puritanism, or more accurately, the more or less evangelical Protestantism, which was so influential in American life until well within the present century—and is not dead yet—our critics of life and manners still have nothing good to say. Heaven knows they can find plenty of ground for complaint. This brand of religion, they may say, was dogmatic, esthetically barren, intellectually obscurantist, given to revivalistic jags, a fertile soil for raising Elmer Gantrys to religious leadership. Ethically it gave religious sanctions to the harsh, unscrupulous, acquisitive code of capitalism, while it placed undue stress upon the morals or unmorals of sex, gambling (off the stock market) and drinking. It must be admitted that these critics can document their case from the records and sometimes from their own memories.

I have no wish nor any intention to argue the case as lawyer for the defense or to pass final judgment from the bench. I speak as one outside the fold of my fathers. No longer do I find adequate, as I once did, the halfway house prepared by modernists who still feel the power of the old traditions as well as the compulsions of the new and confusing day in science, philosophy and social affairs. For good or for evil the religion which was so much and so intimate a part of the life of my boyhood, the religion in which my father's home was founded and nourished, lives for me mostly in memory. To return to it would be an impossible and by no means lovely way of escape from life and its problems.

Yet I think I voice the opinions of many men and women in like case with myself who do not want their children to form their opinion of the faith of their grandfathers from Elmer Gantry or from Mr. Mencken's oft repeated notes on Methodism or from the current judgment of the more voluble of our intelligentsia concerning that from which some of them, like Harry Elmer Barnes, are in conscious and irritated revolt. I should like them to know that there was another side of the picture, that if this devout, rather literalistic, American Protestantism has been weighed in the balance by our generation and found wanting, if palpably it has failed to meet the needs of a world already caught in the toils of revolution, intellectual as well as social, it did at its best nourish men and women worth loving who faced life and death more bravely for their faith.

I am writing out of experience and memory but

what I want to write is not merely and certainly not fully autobiographical. I suspect—indeed I hope—that my generalizations about what their religion meant to my folks will find answering memories in other middle-aged men and women of similar background.

I am the son and grandson of Presbyterian ministers. Their ancestors, mostly country folk, had, I assume, come to America for the usual economic reasons, some of them in early colonial times and some in the first quarter of the nineteenth century. But the family tradition was that some of them had come from France and some from Great Britain to escape actual religious persecution, or at any rate, the burden of an established church. The non-conformist Protestant tradition was strong in our home, but I remember being good friends with our Catholic neighbors. My father spoke in cordial terms of the benign but zealous Catholic priest of our town, and was suspicious of the activities of the A. P. A., the militant anti-Catholic society of that day. As for anti-Semitism, I did not know what it meant until I came across it in a far less religious atmosphere than that in which I was nurtured. Our town went to church and Sunday School but it never regarded Jews or their children as Christ Killers. They were, as I remember it, few in number, but respected not only in the adult community but in that sometimes cruel world which boys set up for themselves and their fellows.

To get back to my grandfathers. One of them died

after a life of toil and some real adventure and hardship as a missionary at home and abroad when I was too young to do more than barely remember him. The other lived until well into his tenth decade, always in full possession of his faculties. His joy and ours was in frequent family reunions of children and grandchildren so that I saw much of him. Until his eightieth year he was a minister in country churches in a lovely, hilly farming region. Every Sunday he made his circuit on horseback or in a buggy over roads which had not yet dreamed of what the coming of the automobile would mean to them.

In these little villages he had brought up and educated, with the mighty aid of a black-eyed and exceedingly capable wife, five children on a salary that I think seldom reached the dizzy heights of $600 yearly. With this he, a farmer's boy, had put himself through college and seminary. His Puritanism was no aid to acquisition!

I do not remember much that he said when he preached but I do remember the little white church, and its cabinet organ and its cheerful bell, and summers with the smell of the country coming in the windows while whole families from the countryside in uncomfortable Sunday best were led to look at life and its sorrows and joys with that mingling of humility and dignity which belonged of right to those chosen to be the children of God. With the years the benediction of peace and sure confidence settled about my grandfather's snow-white head. He, a man of few words, of simple devotion to a stern Calvinistic creed, was "father" to a whole countryside. When an accident from which he amazingly recovered threatened him with a slow and agonizing death, he simply thanked God that of His goodness He permitted him to die "from the feet up rather than from the head down." However far his grandchildren have wandered physically and spiritually, I do not think we shall forget family prayers about his chair nor shall we think of them as any perfunctory superstition or insincere rite. As we sat quietly around him, with his large-type Bible in his lap—one of his few concessions to advancing age—dimly at least we understood from him the sources of a light which gave meaning, yes and glory, to the humdrum task, and all the vicissitudes of the year, a light which bathed, in beauty greater than the sun's, the fields, the shining river, the wooded hills, the cottage and the cherished garden in which this Preacher of the Word lived out his days.

My father lived in larger towns a life outwardly somewhat less placid, and he died before the years had crowned his head with the benedictions his father knew. Yet I think his was a happy life, happy in the love of wife and children and in the respect and confidence of the people to whom he ministered. He was a reserved man who did not wear his heart in his sleeve. He had friends but few intimates. Duty was a great word in his vocabulary, and his code was strict, but we children were not brought up in any atmosphere of gloom. Four times we older children went to church services of various sorts on Sunday, certain books and games and our school studies were taboo that day. I cannot say that I remember the day as one of great joy, but neither was it the thing of horror that I have heard some of my contemporaries describe. There were games and family walks and the atmosphere my mother created which made those Sundays more tolerable than some emancipated youngsters of our generation make their own!

My father was an intelligent and studious man and a preacher far above the average. (I still remember thinking later in life how much I preferred him to preachers of greater fame and far greater concern for publicity!) I never could understand why he seemed so unquestioningly to accept the Calvinist theology which he held. In the retrospect I find it harder to understand how, having accepted it, he was so tolerant of other people. He believed in a hell to which all his life I do not think he ever would say that anyone was bound. I do not believe in his hell and yet have been sorely tempted to consign not a few thereto!

His life, unhurried by modern city standards, was yet far removed from the laziness sometimes associated with the clerical profession. He had a conscience about work as he did about living within his small income and giving generously to church and charity.

My mother was the kind of person who could bring up a large family, help a son with his Latin lesson while getting dinner—and a good one, too—and run various church and civic clubs. She wanted her children to have what she though were the good things of life: health, integrity, education and some cultural opportunities, but for riches as riches she had more of scorn than envy.

I do not mean that there was not some narrowness about the life of the children of the manse; by the compulsions of affection rather than authority we were, most of us, led to eschew dancing, and questions of morals were made to loom perhaps too large in our thinking. The towns in which we lived unquestionably partook of the limitations of Main Street. I was aware that within the Christian Church there could be sorry failures in the Christian graces. And yet as I look backward on the years I remember a happy home with daily proof that marriage can be lasting and beautiful, a home in which there was a non-material standard of values and certainly no sanctimonious hypocrisy. There was, moreover, very little of the suffocating effect of the dogmatic creed my father held. I do not, for instance, remember any drastic censorship on the books we should read.

At least my father's particular brand of orthodoxy did not have room for the antics of Billy Sunday who had plenty of precursors in my boyhood. I remember that some Methodist schoolmates got saved every

year in revivals which were big events in a pre-movie
age. My father believed in an evangelical message to
save souls but not in the emotional orgies which have
had a baleful effect on the American capacity to
think, feel and act sincerely and intelligently in any
province of life.

Now I cannot believe that people like my immediate forebears and experiences like those of my boyhood were unique nor altogether in spite of the
religion which to my parents seemed so important.
Whatever its limitations, that religion at its best gave
some things worth while, some things hard for us to
get from other sources in our troubled times. What
they are or were I think we can distinguish without
great difficulty.

Ethically their religion gave them a code and a conscience which delivered them from the uncertain fu-
tilities of a sophisticated generation without standards
or sense of values. That their code was inadequate I
have already admitted. It made them think too much
of the goodness or badness of men and far too little
of the essential nature of the social system which
held even the best men in its toils. It made them
"Old Testament Christians" accepting at once the
general desirability of peace and the righteousness of
particular wars. Nor were they even discerning in
picking their wars. Intelligent opponents of the war
against Spain and its resultant imperialist struggles
were not recruited from the ranks of evangelical

Protestants. Indeed, the missionary fervor of the churches, honest in itself, fell an easy prey to rationalizations about "manifest destiny" and the "white man's burden." Kipling's "Recessional" was its gospel and the ethics of the "Recessional" were a very poor defense against the machinations of men who gave to the notion of "doing the heathen good" a meaning very different than that which it had in the minds of my forefathers.

Nevertheless the code of the nineteenth century Protestantism at its best was to believers a guide in the maze of life and a deliverer from doubt which greatly conserved their energies and preserved their peace of mind.

It was not, however, in the realm of ethics but of religion in the high sense of relationship to God that the faith of our fathers was a strong tower. We say nowadays, truly, that any strong social conviction, communism for instance, is a religion with many of the faults as well as virtues that we associate with the religious attitude to life. But in its deepest sense religion has always been concerned with the relation of man to the universe. The problem of the existence and nature of God is at the heart of it. Are our noblest aims and ideals and hopes but the illusions of this strange animal man cursed with consciousness in a world essentially alien to his dreams?

For our generation the urgency of such questions can be anesthetized for a longer or shorter time by the compelling problems of economic security and social equality. I often think that the real test of the communist attempt to rid the world of religion will come when—and if—its own achievements as a secular religion of a well-ordered system of production and distribution for the benefit of the workers are fairly secure. What, then, will crowd from the mind of men the old question of the significance of life in a universe made by our science wholly alien to human values, profoundly unconcerned for human destiny?

Already that question stirs our minds—let the popularity of symposiums on science and religion and "living philosophies" bear witness. (Would any other age, I wonder, show such dissimilarities of philosophy, of hope and of despair, among men who share the same culture and the same civilization?) Many of the answers tentatively given are interesting in themselves and provide some antidote against the complete pessimism of Joseph Wood Krutch's *Modern Temper,* but how strange they would seem to the clear assurance of my forefathers!

How they held their theology without its being vitiated by a larger measure of intellectual obscurantism, and a frightened denial of the beginnings of the new science I do not altogether understand. Neither do I know how they escaped the fear of a static immortality of bliss which to us would mitigate the joy of contemplating life eternal. But to a great extent they did these things. They did them, too, with a far deeper sense of the Presence of God, the Father and Friend, than Mr. Walter Lippmann's study of the emphasis on God as King (in his *Preface to Morals*) takes into account.

The result was a sense of meaning, assurance and comfort in life which can scarcely be exaggerated. Evil there was and suffering hard to understand. But over all was God who had His own in His care. His universe was man's home. The generation which believed this did not have to hope with the Bishop of Birmingham that "whatever is at the heart of things is not hostile to our highest aims and ideals." Their God was a Father; not a "whatever is at the heart of things." They would have been far more mystified and puzzled than comforted by Sir Arthur Eddington's dualistic approach to the problem of God and the universe in which many of our own time profess to find consolation. He has written:

"I am convinced that if in physics we pursued to the bitter end an attempt to reach purely objective reality we should simply undo the work of creation and present the world as we might conceive it to have been before the Spirit moved upon the face of the waters. The spiritual element in our experience is the creative element, and if we remove it as we have tried to do in physics on the ground that it also creates illusion, we must ultimately reach the nothingness which was in the beginning."

That is a far cry from the faith in a God who gave

man dominion over the world which He had made
and in that world occasionally had walked and talked
with men. Is not the extraordinary popularity of
Green Pastures in part a testimony to the hunger of
our times for "de Lawd" who can be known and
whose universe man can regard as home?

Whatever wistful hunger of the heart the simplici-
ties of *Green Pastures* may satisfy for a night, our
generation, and still more our children's, must travel
harder roads in its search for truth. But that search
will be more fruitful if we understand what sense of
human dignity and meaning in life our fathers found
in creeds that we may not accept and are often in-
vited to ridicule. Humble and obscure their lives
might have been; they were heirs of life eternal, children of Him who was King of Kings and Lord of
Lords, subjects of His care. That fact helped to rid
them of social fears and base conformity. Their fear
of God left little place for fear of man. I do not
think their heaven was as appalling a place as it sometimes seems to our generation. It was, on the contrary,
a fulfillment of life and an answer to questions otherwise insoluble. The least of them in the world's eyes
might be great in the Kingdom of Heaven. Without
boasting he might say, as did John Bunyan's "Mr.
Valiant for Truth": "My sword, I give to him that
shall succeed me in my Pilgrimage, and my courage
and skill to him that can get it. My marks and scars
I carry with me, that I have fought His battles who

now will be my Rewarder." And of them it could be said as of him: "When the day that he must go hence was come many accompanied him to the river side, into which, as he went, he said: 'Death where is thy sting?' And as he went down deeper he said: 'Grave where is thy victory?' So he passed over, and all the trumpets sounded for him on the other side."

A POSTSCRIPT ON POLITICS

THE essays which make up this book were written in the spring and summer of 1931 and finally edited for publication early in November. Various circumstances somewhat delayed the printing and in the intervening months events marched on—to no safe harbor of peace and plenty. Occasionally by footnotes or the insertion of a sentence I have briefly commented on, or referred to, these more recent developments. Some of them are of such importance as to deserve fuller mention lest the reader question their effect on the drift of our times that I have been discussing.

In substance, I see no reason for altering the judgments I have expressed. We drift, and we drift toward disaster. There is a tragic amount of misery and great discontent in the United States but no proportionate amount of action, wise or otherwise. The docility of labor is even more amazing than it seemed last summer. This greatest of depressions has thus far produced no such demonstrations as did the depressions of the seventies and nineties.

Politically there are no signs of the emergence of a working class mass movement which will give us an effective new "third party" in the 1932 campaign. There is a greatly increased interest in socialism.

Aside from that, there are local and sporadic revivals of populism. The difficulty new and financially weak parties will find in getting on the ballot in any considerable number of states of itself will probably block the appearance of any sort of new third party on a national scale.

Financial considerations, above all the great cost of a modern campaign, doubtless help to account for the conservatism of the Democrats. Their party still has more to fear or hope from business interests than from labor. The winning slogan for the party, gravely approved by three prominent Democratic Senators, was "Hee, haw, we're coming back"—a slogan characteristic of a party without principle and possibly without intelligence.

In domestic affairs Democrats coöperated with Republicans in passing the President's pet Reconstruction Finance Corporation bill, to which I have previously alluded in a footnote. Some such bill was doubtless necessary to prevent a complete collapse of the banking system. Such a bill should have tended to deflate swollen capitalization while tending to maintain or increase wages, thus aiding the purchasing power of the masses and an increase of consumption. All sound economics point that way. Only the immediate selfish interest of an owning class is opposed. Yet that interest won and the bill went wrong. Both its terms and the personnel of its administration make it virtually certain that the operation of the Reconstruction Finance law will do more for security holders than workers. Unemployed workers, now that banks and railroads, etc., are cared for, may get some federal aid which, fortunately, the A. F. of L. is demanding. But there is no sign of a half-way adequate and comprehensive program of unemployment amelioration, Democratic or Republican.

In discussing foreign affairs two leading contenders for the Democratic presidential nomination in varying degrees have declared a moratorium or turned their backs on the one principle they ever had!— loyalty to the League of Nations. This is only one proof of the power of the dogma of international isolation in America. Another and more dangerous proof is the action of Congress in serving notice that it will not consider cancellation of interallied debts on any terms. Doubtless a referendum in America would overwhelmingly endorse this stand, while a second referendum would endorse tariff and other policies which make it virtually impossible for our debtors to pay their debts!

Suspicion of the League of Nations plus a desire for whatever trade advantages Japan's imperialism in Manchuria might bring, made America hold back rather than take the lead in urging an international embargo on loans or shipments of war supplies to a nation which flouted all machinery for peace. Instead we became increasingly benevolent to Japan's Manchurian invasion—so like our own Western imperialism in its motives and its alleged justification! As the New York *Times* editorially admitted, the world was resigned to the Manchurian adventure until the amazing madness of the military clique in control in Japan added the Shanghai attack to it.

As I write, so acute is the Shanghai situation that not only are its guns likely to drown out the prayers of the masses for disarmament at Geneva, but they may even precipitate a new world war itself. Yet there are evidences that Japan, whose domestic finances are in bad shape and whose military forces find Chinese resistance unexpectedly strong at Shanghai, may have to draw back. Its government, backed probably by popular sentiment (but with the principal radical leaders in jail) is still imperialistic in demands. It seeks, however, to associate with it the western powers in "demilitarizing" the principal Chinese ports. To the stark dismemberment of China, America must never give assent. But on no condition and by no "incident" which our military display in Shanghai invites, must we be drawn into a senseless war against Japan. In the long run China and the Chinese can take care of themselves. We can give aid by moral and financial pressure, not by military action which will repeat the ancient madness of pouring out the blood of millions of the innocent to vindicate an abstraction like the honor of the flag. If the government will not act, a popular boycott in America of Japanese goods may be salutary.

Meanwhile at Geneva or afterwards pressure for disarmament must go on. Nor can disarmament be tied up with an armed League of Nations to enforce "security" which France through André Tardieu has formally suggested. The present state of the world makes that preposterous.

Both in foreign and domestic affairs our banking interests appear in a worse light than even last summer. Wall Street, as revealed by the Senate's investigation, snapped up dubious foreign loans and dumped them under pressure on weak banks and uninformed Main Street investors. One bad Peruvian loan was got by paying the son of her former president a cool half million which was nothing but a bribe! Newspaper estimates, based on testimony brought out by Senator Hiram Johnson, show that Wall Street bankers made upwards of $120,000,000 on loans that have already lost the American people two billion dollars.

But this does not mean, as Senator Johnson would have us think, that therefore we must under no circumstances aid the nefarious bankers by forgiving the war debts. To cling to the war debts is not to punish primarily the bankers for their sins in the matter of foreign loans or their equal sins in our own domestic stock flotations. It is to punish the workers of the world.

There are signs, as I have previously said, that capitalism throughout the world, including the bankers, will swallow some losses and turn fascist with a great emphasis on nationalism to hypnotize the workers. Socialists must remain internationalist. Neither in the matter of war debts, tariffs, aid to dumping cotton or grain abroad, nor in fiscal policy can we seek to bribe temporarily the farmers and workers by unsound measures of a sort now popular.

Our socialist task was never clearer. It is first of all to promote the socialist philosophy or view of life. It is to hold up the vision of the classless society to the workers of the world, a society from which poverty and war are forever banished. Save on the basis of this socialist philosophy there is no hope for any tactics or program, whether of war or peace, dictatorship or democracy, to succeed.

Next comes a program some parts of which must be immediately applicable. Less and less am I enthused about the "ultimate" salvation of a world in which the next generation or generations must go through hell. Such salvation seems to me almost as remote as a Utopia on Mars. It is, moreover, dubious of attainment. Wretched, half-starved children are not the builders of a beautiful coöperative commonwealth. Never was mere revolt, however justified, less likely to succeed in building the new order than today. Hence the need of programs of unemployment amelioration, of decent housing, of agricultural aid and proper taxation of incomes and inheritances, not to galvanize a dying order into a little longer life, but to give us men with vigor to build the new society. Hence the need of plans for socializing power and other public utilities and natural resources, not as isolated panaceas but as steps in a comprehensive plan of socialism. As much as any populist we are concerned with money, banking and credit. We doubt the various populist patent medicines of bimetalism or uncontrolled inflation. We know the need of a managed currency not bound to the fetish of gold or silver, but we know that this also must, to be effective, be part of a plan for the socialization of basic wealth and the social control of fundamental economic policies.

We shall not be saved by paper plans. All our hopes and vision and knowledge will be in vain if we remain side-line critics or a mere sect of true believers. The Five Year plan the Socialist Party in America needs most is a five year plan to build on sound lines its own organization. I am convinced that it can be done. No better or greater organization is in sight. Our task will require intelligence, effort, sacrifice. It will require, especially of our younger men and women on whom we must depend, an end of a once popular cynicism, or of a too great absorption in minor points of doctrine. It will require enlistment for life in the great crusade. We may differ in tactics, but on one thing facts compel us to agree: in the struggle in which we are caught there can be no true neutrality. He that is not with the workers is against them. One thing or the other. Either by action or passivity we shall aid an owning class in trying to prolong a system which is the mother of poverty and insecurity, of soul destroying exploitation and war, or else we shall be of the army of the workers who seek to create the federation of the coöperative commonwealths of mankind in which peace and plenty shall be the universal heritage, and freedom and fellowship the law of life.